Quarterly Essay

CONTENTS

1   POWER TRIP
    The Political Journey of Kevin Rudd
    David Marr

93 CORRESPONDENCE
    John Hirst, George Brandis, Tom Switzer, Andrew Norton, George Megalogenis, Jean Curthoys, Martin Krygier, Waleed Aly

137 Contributors

Quarterly Essay is published four times a year by Black Inc., an imprint of Schwartz Media Pty Ltd. Publisher: Morry Schwartz.

ISBN 978-1-86395-477-8   ISSN 1832-0953

ALL RIGHTS RESERVED.
No part of this publication may be reproduced, stored in a retrieval system, or transmitted in any form by any means electronic, mechanical, photocopying, recording or otherwise without the prior consent of the publishers.

Essay & correspondence © retained by the authors.

Subscriptions – 1 year (4 issues): $49 within Australia incl. GST. Outside Australia $79.
2 years (8 issues): $95 within Australia incl. GST. Outside Australia $155.
Payment may be made by Mastercard or Visa, or by cheque made out to Schwartz Media. Payment includes postage and handling.

To subscribe, fill out and post the subscription card, or subscribe online at:

www.quarterlyessay.com

Correspondence and subscriptions should be addressed to the Editor at:

Black Inc. Level 5, 289 Flinders Lane
Melbourne VIC 3000 Australia
Phone: 61 3 9654 2000 / Fax: 61 3 9654 2290
Email:
quarterlyessay@blackincbooks.com (editorial)
subscribe@blackincbooks.com (subscriptions)

Editor: Chris Feik. Management: Sophy Williams, Caitlin Yates. Publicity: Elisabeth Young. Design: Guy Mirabella. Assistant Editor: Adam Shaw. Typesetting: Duncan Blachford.

Printed by Griffin Press, Australia. The paper used to produce this book comes from wood grown in sustainable forests.

POWER TRIP

The Political Journey of Kevin Rudd

David Marr

WONDERFUL, WONDERFUL

"Those Chinese fuckers are trying to rat-fuck us," declared Kevin Rudd. As snow fell on Copenhagen – on its palaces and squats, on police and their dogs, on protesters rugged up against the fierce cold and on the big, bland Bella Center where the largest gathering of world leaders in history sulked and plotted – the prime minister of Australia faced the collapse of old dreams. This was the little boy fascinated by China, the kid who longed to be a diplomat, the man who believed a better world might be built through international agreement, and a prime minister struggling to meet "one of the greatest moral, economic and environmental challenges of our age." Life had brought him, inevitably it seemed, to this icy Scandinavian city a few days before Christmas 2009 and he blamed the Chinese for wrecking it all.

The Copenhagen that mattered began on 17 December and lasted forty hours. Rudd slept for one of them. He wasn't shy. He relished working with the big boys. Almost to the very end he was a player in the meetings that mattered. He began the last long haul working with Gordon Brown to try to persuade low-lying states like Kiribati and the Maldives to let the world warm a little more than 1.5 degrees. Mid-morning saw him deliver his set speech to the full plenary in the big hall. It was superior Rudd – pared down, not too much jargon, only a little mawkish about Gracie:

> Before I left Australia, I was presented with a book of handwritten letters from a group of six-year-olds. One of the letters is from Gracie. Gracie is six. "Hi," she wrote. "My name is Gracie. How old are you?" Gracie continues, "I am writing to you because I want you all to be strong in Copenhagen. Please listen to us as it is our future." I fear that at this conference, we are on the verge of letting little Gracie down.

Australians with sharp ears might have picked the trademark boast that Rudd had done his homework: "If you examine, as I have done, the 102 square bracketed areas of disagreement that lie in the existing text before us …"

After Queen Margrethe's state dinner at the Christiansborg Palace – Rudd so monopolised Princess Mary's attentions that the British prime minister on her other side was left staring at his plate – he joined Nicolas Sarkozy, Angela Merkel, Brown and another twenty world leaders in free-wheeling and futile efforts to find agreement. At 3 a.m. they left the haggling to their environment ministers. By this time delegates were sleeping on sofas all over the Bella Center. Rudd had an hour's kip in an armchair, all he felt he needed to keep going.

Barack Obama jetted into the city that morning and joined the talks. The United States was offering little in the way of emissions cuts but wanted what the president called accountability. "Without any accountability, any agreement would be empty words on a page," Obama told the delegates. Absent was Wen Jiabao. The snub was deliberate. Rudd believed the Chinese were intent on sabotaging any deal that involved binding obligations and international monitoring.

Tired and exasperated, surrounded by a knot of Australian officials and press, Rudd began to rage against the Chinese. He needed sleep. His anger was real, but his language seemed forced, deliberately foul. In this mood, he'd been talking about countries "rat-fucking" each other for days. Was a deal still possible, asked one of the Australians. "Depends whether those rat-fucking Chinese want to fuck us."

Obama postponed his departure a few hours. At nightfall on an already endless day, the leaders of the twenty-six nations met again, with Wen Jiabao once more pointedly absent. The *Guardian*'s Mark Lynas reported the Chinese blocking every initiative:

> "Why can't we even mention our own targets?" demanded a furious Angela Merkel. Australia's prime minister, Kevin Rudd, was annoyed enough to bang his microphone.

The bones of the Copenhagen Accord were decided that evening in a meeting between the US, China, India, Brazil and South Africa. Rudd was not there. The leaders agreed to vague targets, no monitoring and more gatherings down the track. This bare deal was sent on to Rudd's group of leaders. Meanwhile Obama briefed the US press and flew out on *Air Force One*. When Rudd emerged an hour later, he had to be told the world already knew the outcome. Addressing reporters with barely the energy to take notes, he declared bravely: "We prevailed. Some will be disappointed by the amount of progress. The alternative was, frankly, catastrophic collapse of these negotiations."

His efforts at Copenhagen are Rudd's answer to those who accuse him of being a bureaucrat at heart, an incrementalist, a leader unable to dream. He sees Copenhagen as proof that he's willing to go out on a limb, spend political capital and court trouble at home for a great cause. And Rudd insists Copenhagen was not a failure. He is one of an unusual species: the diplomat turned leader. Though his time in the foreign service was a brief seven years, they've marked him for life. For the diplomat, negotiations have never failed so long as there's a prospect, however vague, of agreement somewhere down the track. For someone who thinks as he does, it can be just as important to keep everyone at the table, to keep talks going, to keep hopes alive, as it is to bring great issues to a head. The rhetoric of success Rudd used in these exhausted hours wasn't all spin. It was authentic Rudd.

That he was still on his feet seemed a miracle. This least athletic of men has deep emotional and physical resilience. His climate-change minister, Penny Wong, was dead on her feet. Rudd seemed unaware of this. He was taken aside and urged to get her out of there, to get her to her hotel. Wong found a shower somewhere and stayed on for the last session. Later that morning Copenhagen came to a formal end, with the parties merely "noting" the vague deal brokered by Obama and Wen Jiabao.

Rudd's bond with the people began to fray after Copenhagen. Having picked him as a leader long before he became his party's choice, Australians had held Rudd in extraordinary affection for years. Never had the polls shown a prime minister so popular for so long. But after this debacle the mood shifted. Malcolm Turnbull had fallen. His place as leader of the Opposition was taken by a Tory head-kicker unembarrassed to embrace the denialists' cause. The old consensus on climate change, which Rudd had identified himself with so closely, began to melt away. In April this year when he abandoned his emissions trading scheme until the far reaches of a second term, the people and the polls turned on him savagely. His leadership was in question. Rudd had sold himself to the Australian people as a new kind of leader: a man of intellect and values out to reshape the future. If he isn't that, people are asking, what is he? And who is he? Rudd seems to have been with us forever yet still be a newcomer, indeed a stranger, in the Lodge. Millions of words have been written about him since he emerged from the Labor pack half-a-dozen years ago, but Rudd remains hidden in full view.

If Australia saw him through Canberra's eyes, he would be done for. Though he has led until now a formidably disciplined first-term government – few leaks, only one minister lost – negotiated the global banking crisis of 2008 with exemplary skill, pulled off the great symbolic coup of the Apology and routed two Opposition leaders, the capital is tired of him. He's seen in that little world of power as a weird guy and a failing prime minister. He puzzles his caucus, frustrates his ministers and irritates the press. The *Australian* has turned on him with a determination often as comic as it's brutal. He is accused of running a chaotic office and bullying public servants. A habit of making endless speeches at big public events has earned the man – known at various times in his career as Dr Death, Pixie, Harry Potter and Heavy Kevvie – a new nickname: the Castro of the South Pacific.

When his approval rating began to dip sharply in the polls early this year, commentators wondered if he might be the first prime minister since Scullin back in the Depression to lose power after only a single term. There was speculation that he was in a very delicate position: essentially friendless in the party and ripe for decapitation by Julia Gillard even before the looming elections. This is rubbish. For one thing it underestimates the debts owed by the party to only the third man in sixty years to bring Labor from Opposition to government. But such talk does point to the strange patterns of the man's political career.

He is not Labor's leader because he reshaped the party around him as Gough Whitlam did. Nor was he a favourite son like Bob Hawke. Nor did he wrest the leadership after long internal warfare as Paul Keating did. Rudd leads no faction in the party and has won few friends in caucus. His rise to power was a peculiar triumph over his own party's opposition – indeed, derision – achieved by appealing directly to the Australian people. Rudd's dominance in the party is first and foremost about the polls.

Leaders aren't there to be liked. Being an arsehole is no bar to high office. They always disappoint. The public understands this. And people know the climb to power can be bloody. Such things are forgiven if it all proves worthwhile. But of Rudd it has to be said that there is a large number of people who, having worked with him as a diplomat, public servant, shadow minister, leader of the Opposition or lately as prime minister, loathe the man. Between the verdicts of the public and those who come to know him face to face, there is a curiously wide gulf. It's narrowing fast. Mark Latham once told him that he only held his position in the party "because of his media profile and public standing among people who have never actually met him." That's characteristically cruel, but it points to the fundamental question about Rudd that remains unanswered: who is he?

Colleagues from his time as the key back-room boy in Wayne Goss's reforming government have an old joke they trot out whenever they meet to talk about those days of high hopes and disappointment. They don't remember Rudd kindly. The joke: he is a creature from outer space. The proof? Who but an android would say so often, "I am only human."

EUMUNDI LOST

On 14 December 1968, Bert Rudd drove his white Rambler down to Brisbane for an afternoon of indoor bowls followed by a dinner at the Buffalo Temple in Fortitude Valley. He drank beer and whiskey at both. Driving home alone to the farm where 120 cows would be waiting to be milked in the morning, he hit a telegraph pole near Caboolture. The impact ruptured his spleen. He was taken to Royal Brisbane Hospital where he died of septicaemia eight weeks later.

His son Kevin was eleven. For a long time, he wouldn't tell the story of the bad years that followed his father's death. That he'd grown up a dreamy barefoot kid on a dairy farm was no secret, but what happened then was something friends and colleagues knew little or nothing about. They didn't ask questions. They sensed his childhood was a no-go zone. Rudd was forty-five and beginning his run for the leadership of the Labor Party before he began talking of the events that still drive his plain, conservative politics. That long silence says much about Rudd's pride. Until it became necessary to speak about those hard years, he thought them better forgotten. He wanted to be known for what he had become and what he had achieved rather than the mess his family found itself in when he was a boy. He couldn't claim the Rudds had suffered a uniquely terrible tragedy. Others had it much worse. So secret was the family's past that when the dire circumstances of his early years provoked a political hullabaloo before the elections of 2007, there were cousins in the hills round Nambour who had never heard of the hardship Marge Rudd and the kids endured after Bert's death.

Nambour was a place of secrets and high expectations, where respectable families didn't complain, worked hard and got on with things. Sugar, milk and government were the business of a town dominated, as it had been for the best part of a century, by the chimney of the sugar mill and the Methodist church – first weatherboard and then brick – on Maud Street. "The drive to create strong civic, commercial and educational institutions flowed strongly through the Nambour burghers' blood and spirit," argued Professor Michael Wesley in *Griffith Review*. "Sober men with stubborn jaws" set the rules the town still lived by. New people were pouring in, but the old families ran the place:

> This fostered the flipside of Nambour's dynamism – the steady stream of people who left. Many who left had absorbed the town's gifts – its cheerful optimism, strong traditions of schooling excellence, public health facilities – but also felt stifled by its proprieties, snobbishness and low horizons.

Rudd's mother Margaret (Marge) De Vere was a well-spoken, fussy, hard-working, teetotal Catholic who trained as a nurse during the War. Her father had taken up farming after first drinking the profits of the Commercial Hotel in Currie Street. The politics of the family were conservative but mixed. Her brothers were solid Country Party: Eddie was Nambour's mayor for years and the other Kevin in the family was chairman of Gympie Shire. Small-town politics was in the blood. Her children would grow up with close family connections to the political machine that ran Queensland. But her own politics were even more conservative: Labor until the great Split of 1954, after which she cast her vote for the Catholic Church-backed Democratic Labor Party for forty years.

Bert Rudd was a blow-in from New South Wales who came to the district with a mate after the War. The Rudds – no relation to "Steele Rudd," creator of Dad and Dave – were from way down the heap: Protestant fettlers and rural labourers from around Wagga. Convict stock. Bert and Marge met at a dance and married in the Catholic Church in 1948. Bert didn't convert. He remained, like so many in the district, a keen member of the Buffalo Lodge. A first son, Malcolm, was born swiftly in 1949; a daughter, Loree, followed in 1950; another son, Gregory, came a few years later; and baby Kevin appeared in September 1957. By the most perfect coincidence Labor lost power that week to the Country Party in Queensland. Rudd would be intimately involved in the party's return to office thirty-two years later.

The Rudds were living in a neat little house on a low rise outside the village of Eumundi. Bert was share-farming for Aubrey Low, the milk and butter Czar of the district. Kevin was sickly and lived in the protective embrace of his mother. An operation at the age of three to correct his badly bowed legs left him having to learn to walk again. Sometime between the age of five and seven he was struck down by rheumatic fever and he found himself once again in hospital and recuperating at home for long stretches. That the fever had affected his heart was not discovered for half-a-dozen years. The damaged heart was on a list of dark Rudd secrets that would only emerge in a Liberal Party smear campaign before the 2007 poll. Did he have the ticker?

The boy was a fussy little dreamer. He had a horse and wandered barefoot to the local primary school, but nothing much was expected of him round the farm: "I was the last in the litter and most of the hard work was done by those who came before me," he told Julia Baird on ABC radio. His sister, Loree, remembers him lost in his own world: "When he was young, he preferred to design castles out of the cow feed in the huge feed-box at the centre of the dairy rather than actually run diligently with the stuff to feed-boxes between cow rotations." His brother Greg complained of sharing a room with a little brother who nagged him about being messy. "Is it so hard," the child would ask, "to pick up those socks and put them in that drawer?" Rudd remembers as a small boy being woken before dawn by his knockabout father to be taken on the Anzac Day march: "I always remember in the dim, very early morning light, hearing the gentle clink of medals." Bert still clung to the idea that little Kevin would grow up to be a farmer. "Have you made up your mind?" he asked his ten-year-old one day as they stared down the road. "Is it going to be beef or is it going to be dairy?"

Marge had other plans. She had him learning the piano, turning up at the Eumundi School of Arts in fancy dress – a Chinaman one day and Rubens' Blue Boy another – and taking ballroom dancing classes. As prime minister he confessed: "I grew up in a Queensland where it was perfectly acceptable for a ten-year-old boy to dance the 'Pride of Erin' for recreation." Into her child's dream world she dropped a book on archaeology. Of the handful of details about his early life Rudd has always been happy to give – the carefree years on the farm, loving parents, an old horse – this is curiously potent: a book about the ancient world with one chapter on China that brought its emperors and armies, temples and palaces to life.

Marge Rudd raised her children Catholic. She took them to mass every Sunday and catechism every second Saturday. "Mum would bellow out the window of the farmhouse across the flats, 'It's time for catechism,'" Rudd told his biographer Robert Macklin. "She had a habit of being able to round you up pretty quickly and get you in there." She and the children said the rosary together in her bedroom on Sunday nights as Bert watched *Disneyland*.

Her faith was strong and individual. She did not go to confession, assuring the priests she made a clean breast of her sins directly to God. She was not sectarian. The moral lessons she taught her children were drawn as often as not from the good example of Protestant worthies of the district. Hers was an "old-style Queensland rural Catholic Country Women's Association" faith, her son would say: "If you saw someone in distress you couldn't be indifferent to that, you had to do something about it." The church's teaching on social justice did not interest her. Rudd did not absorb at her knee the words of Leo XIII's *Rerum Novarum* on the failings of brute capitalism. She wasn't one to bother with Papal encyclicals.

Her God could be cruel. Marge Rudd's favourite passage of the Bible has the Lord tending his vines with secateurs:

> Every branch in me that beareth not fruit he taketh away: and every branch that beareth fruit, he purgeth it, that it may bring forth more fruit … if a man abide not in me, he is cast forth as a branch, and is withered; and men gather them, and cast them into the fire, and they are burned.

Perhaps in this teaching of destruction and renewal she was able to accommodate the calamity that befell the family in the summer of 1968 when her husband crashed the new Rambler outside Caboolture. Her youngest boy had lately turned eleven and she had stayed behind in Eumundi to watch him perform at the Christmas party of the kids' ballroom dancing class in the School of Arts. News of the crash came through to the farmhouse in the early hours of the morning. Most of the next eight weeks she spent at her husband's bedside in Royal Brisbane Hospital. Her youngest boy shuttled back and forth as Bert slowly died. "There were great concerns about the calibre of the surgeons who were operating on him toward the end," Rudd told *Sixty Minutes*' Ellen Fanning nearly thirty years later. He was convinced it was not the crash but the wretched state of Queensland's hospitals that killed his father.

Eumundi has come a long way since then. The dairy farms have gone. Kids wear shoes to school. The Berkelouw brothers have opened one of their swish bookshops on Eumundi Memorial Drive. But all these years later the town is still divided over the fate of the Rudds after Bert's death. The parties have now gone to ground. One of farmer Low's daughters, Jill McCone, had her Sydney solicitors warn me off: I was to cease trying to contact their client. They told me in Eumundi, where Low is remembered as an old drunk who wove down the roads in big American cars, "You'll never get to the truth around here."

Bert Rudd was a sharefarmer. The house came with the job. That Marge Rudd and her children had to leave after his death is not really in dispute. Even so, the departure was humiliating for the mother and child. The boy would later say that being thrown off the farm – the Narnia of his childhood – caused him more anguish than his father's death. He called it *eviction* and told the *Women's Weekly* it came swift and hard:

> Within two or three weeks of Dad's funeral, we were told we had to go ... I can remember the terrible discussion between my mother and the fellow who owned the land. That was really tough

for Mum – my two brothers were away at school and she had me and my sister, Loree, to care for, but Mum handled herself well and off we went.

But according to McCone, the Rudds' departure was slow and considerate, not the work of a ruthless landlord but the natural order of things in the bush. She told the *Sun-Herald*'s Kerry-Anne Walsh:

> Margaret would always have known at some point, inevitably, an incoming farmer would have to occupy the farmhouse. But provisions were put in place by our father for Margaret. He explained to her she could remain on the farm, at no cost whatsoever, until such time as the new farmer arrived ... to continuously say he was evicted immediately after his dad's funeral is quite an unbelievable statement. Not only does he blame our father for the so-called eviction, he subsequently mentions having to sleep rough in a car.

Rudd responded furiously when the *Sun-Herald* alerted him in early March 2007 to its scoop. He took it he was being accused of lying and set out, in the words of the *Sydney Morning Herald*'s Alan Ramsey, to kill the story: "And when I say kill, I mean kill. Not deferred, or gutted, or rewritten to suit the Labor leader. Gone altogether. Kaput. Never published."

After a number of abusive calls from Rudd's staff, the paper's editor, Simon Dulhunty, gave him a week's reprieve and sent a journalist north to Eumundi. News next weekend that the story was going ahead reached the leader of the Opposition as he was lunching at the house of the *Daily Telegraph* columnist Piers Akerman. His staff rang and abused Dulhunty. Then Rudd rang and many harsh things were said – e.g. "You're kicking my dead mother in the guts" – in a call that lasted at least half an hour. Dulhunty told Ramsey:

> Rudd kept insisting the story shouldn't run. He hung up, but called back again, asserting that to publish would be "a serious mistake," it wasn't right, it was "an assault" on his character. "Cut to the core,

Simon," he said. "This is nothing about anyone else, it's not the story of a family's interpretation of events, this is an assault on my character. Cut to the core."

When the shouting died down, Rudd dictated a dignified reply to the Lows' claims that appeared next day in the paper. It was all he had ever needed to say in the first place:

> Mr Low got on well with my father and I understand was well respected in the wider community – but he was a tough, very tough businessman, as my mother discovered in her dealings with him after my father's death. I understand that the Low family will want to honour their father's story and the good things I am sure that he did for the wider community, but when it comes to his business dealings with my mum after my dad's death, it is exactly as I have described. Others from the time have exactly the same recollection.

Rudd had made a hash of things. His determination to micro-manage the story left the public with exactly the impression he was desperate to avoid: of being caught peddling a fake hard-luck yarn to win public sympathy. Two truths emerge from this spat. He has a glass jaw. And the loss of his childhood paradise on the edge of Eumundi is a wound that has never healed.

The Rudds were suddenly poor, with only the charity of their De Vere relatives to fall back on – "I didn't find that a terribly dignifying experience," said Rudd – so his mother found a job in a nursing home at Scarborough on the Redcliffe peninsula outside Brisbane. The boy was farmed out to neighbours to finish the term at Eumundi primary, then followed her south. After a brief stint at a local De La Salle school, the little boy turned up halfway through 1969 as a boarder at Marist College Ashgrove in the Brisbane hills. He was a charity case: the school met the bills because Marge Rudd was known as a good Catholic. At about this time, she moved into the Mater Hospital in Brisbane to begin a year's retraining as a nurse.

Ashgrove marked Rudd. He emerged with an icy hatred of the school. "It was tough, harsh, unforgiving, institutional Catholicism of the old school," he told Julia Baird. "I didn't like it." Was there physical abuse, she asked. "Some of the Brothers whacked kids and some were actually quite kind, but it was still the culture, I think it's fair to say – and others would agree with me – which condoned violence." Not all the Brothers were quite in control of themselves. Old boys talk of Brothers beating children for no clear reason in a paroxysm of rage. They seemed to pick on the weak and the lonely. Nor were threats of sexual abuse entirely absent. "Some of the Brothers had a dubious affection for their young charges," Cosima Marriner reported in the *Sydney Morning Herald*. "Former students can still remember the Brother who would always volunteer for shower duty."

The day began at Ashgrove with mass at six. But the other religion of the school was rugby. Everyone had to play. There was cricket in summer and long cross-country runs which left Rudd trailing far behind. He tried to keep up but couldn't. A medical examination revealed his damaged heart. At the age of twelve, his status as a sickly child was confirmed. He was invisible to his classmates. Though he showed some promise at the piano, his schoolwork was mediocre. Each night this prissy kid who had lost his father and was separated from his mother found himself living, in the words of his brother Greg, "in a dorm with fifty guys farting and their smelly socks." Plus the Brothers on patrol.

Holidays were difficult. Now that his mother was training at the Mater, they had no home base and the boy was conscious of being passed "from pillar to post" as they moved between friends and De Vere relatives: "You've always got to be polite and you know you're not quite part of who you're staying with, you're only there temporarily." On perhaps two or three occasions there was nowhere for them to stay. Marge pulled the VW Beetle over to the side of the road and they slept in the car. The boy thought to himself: "It doesn't get much crooker than this."

He escaped Ashgrove after two years. His mother, having finished her training, found a job in Nambour at the Selangor Private Hospital, bought a fibro cottage round the corner and brought her boy home in the winter of 1971. Rudd has never since encouraged Ashgrove to claim him as its own. "I prefer not to remember those days," he told a Brisbane lawyer in the 1990s. "I received my education at Nambour High." Over the course of that lunch he left this distinguished Ashgrove old boy "in no doubt that he detested the joint." Last year Rudd sent on DVD an official message of staggering rudeness to mark the opening of a new science block named after his old headmaster. Sitting in front of a few shelves of Hansard and an Australian flag, Rudd mangled the man's name, reminded Ashgrove's old boys more than once that he was prime minister and subjected them to a brief stump speech about Labor's contribution to science education across the nation. His scorn was colossal.

The move to Nambour High in September 1971 was not an immediate success. This jumble of classrooms on the low side of Coronation Avenue was the boy's fourth school in three years. He arrived there a little fearful of what might befall him as he once again finessed his way around a strange playground. But back home under his mother's protective care, he soon found his feet. He was always his mother's son.

That was the year Gough Whitlam visited China. The boy was glued to the set, mesmerised by the sight of the Labor leader being feted in Beijing. Even at the age of thirteen he sensed he was watching a great man at an extraordinary moment: "What leadership!" Rudd was sixteen when Whitlam returned to Beijing as prime minister. Again he was transfixed. "I watched with wide eyes on the flickering tube Gough and Margaret embark on their triumphal march to China in 1973. I read every word about who Gough met and what was said at his meeting with Zhou Enlai and Mao Zedong." This was not the enthusiasm of a Labor neophyte. Rudd had yet to make contact with the family that would transform his politics. Whitlam's adventures in China meant something more fundamental than that:

> As a kid growing up in the Queensland country under the occasionally benign, but more often malign, Bjelke-Petersen dictatorship of the 1970s, it was Gough who opened this person's eyes to the world beyond, by which I mean not just beyond the Tweed – radical though that was at the time as the Tweed, in those days, constituted our very own Mason–Dixon Line – but the region beyond our shores …

By this time the gears had meshed. When school resumed the following year – 1974, his last at Nambour – the teachers discovered a boy implacably determined to succeed. "I have never met a mind like Kevin Rudd's in forty years of teaching," recalls Fae Barber. "He was cherubic, sitting in the front row just waiting to absorb knowledge. To this day, I love and admire him." And he counts her one of the great influences on his life. He immersed himself in his work. He read. He questioned. He imaginatively entered the worlds Barber took him to: literature and ancient history. "I remember teaching him about Caesar's troubles with Pompey the Great, and young Kevin was *angered* by Pompey's poor behaviour."

This was more than mere swotting. He was determined to rebuild himself from the ground up. This would be a new Kevin Rudd, not the vulnerable kid who had suffered what he called "a deep sense of loss of dignity" since the family was thrown off the farm. Not the boy who had been shocked by the violence of Ashgrove. With steely determination he would rise above the wrongs of these past years and make a big life for himself. The aim was to become unassailable. And he began to see this determination to remake himself as having a larger purpose. "I just got determined to make sure that I could look after myself in life," he told Julia Baird. "And do something about what I saw to be wrong things happening in the world."

BABE IN THE WOODS

Rudd found Labor almost by accident. Among his few friends at Nambour High were the Callander girls. They remember him as an awkward kid. "When he was up on his feet and talking, he was most comfortable in his own skin," says Fiona Callander (now Neucom). "But he was not a confident person in a social situation. He was not the life and soul of the party." They brought him home to their pineapple farm where he met their father, Bob. Twenty-five years later in his maiden speech Rudd would acknowledge that "Bob Callander … introduced me to the Australian Labor Party."

This prince of the newsroom had decided at the age of forty to abandon his career at the Sydney *Sun* and grow pineapples. So entirely unlikely and so doomed was this venture that for years journalists at Fairfax were warned to watch out when turning forty "not to do a Callander." Dashing, fashionable and larger than life, he had reported from London and the Middle East, was right there on the Darwin tarmac when the KGB tried to hustle Mrs Petrov onto her plane, and had risen almost to the top of one of Sydney's big afternoon papers. He was also a friend to young talent. Peter Barron, who went on to greatness in Kerry Packer's empire, was a Callander protégé. So was the young Kerry O'Brien.

The decision to give all this away was largely dictated by his doctors. After some nasty bouts of pancreatitis, Callander had given up the grog and was anxious to break with the hard-drinking culture of the press that was killing his friends. On the wagon and looking for fresh adventures, he took his family north to Woombye on the outskirts of Nambour and watched his first pineapples rot in the floods of 1972. The great consolation of that year was the election of his hero Gough Whitlam. Callander's daughter Kerry says: "Politics is what made him tick."

Callander was the first Labor man Rudd was ever aware of meeting. He was a raconteur and the boy lapped up his stories. "Kevin was an absolute babe in the woods, but Dad could see his potential," recalls Fiona

Neucom. "Dad would bait him in a joking way to open his mind. He didn't like to see a brain go to waste, and anyone with a brain like Kevin's voting for the National Party would really be going to waste."

With the Callanders he went to his first political meeting: Bjelke-Petersen addressing a packed Nambour Town Hall in the Queensland campaign of 1974. The Callanders didn't stand for the national anthem. Rudd did. He was a good boy. He was at the Callanders' to watch television on election night and see Labor reduced to a cricket team in the state parliament. But it was so exciting to be there with Bob: he knew the people up on the screen.

At some point that year Rudd had begun dropping in on Young Labor meetings at the Nambour Cane Growers' Hall on Lowe Street. The first speaker to address them was that old fossil Senator George Georges. The boy did not join the party. There was a small kerfuffle at school when he conducted a voter survey in the playground. Support for Labor was running at a dispiriting 28 per cent. Later press stories of him clashing with authorities over his new political beliefs are exaggerated. He told me he was only ever asked to remove a Young Labor sticker from his clipboard. "He never did anything to get into trouble at school," says Barber. "He was the one with the halo."

Nambour's service clubs, a legacy of the town's ethos of self-improvement, were to prove more important to the boy in this formative last year at school than Young Labor. To the Jaycees, the Lions and Rotary, he delivered his set piece: "Australia – The Democracy." The Nambour *Chronicle* reported an early version of this work in progress:

> Kevin said the present apathy on the part of many voters, and the "donkey" vote, could only be overcome by the dissemination of a workable knowledge of the subject of government in such a form as to be comprehendable to the man in the street. He called attention to the fact that no compulsory provisions exist for a student to obtain even an elementary knowledge of this subject at school.

> He advocated that the subject of government be introduced to school curricula, which would entail an examination of the policies of major parties and the structure of government.

Marge Rudd drove him more than a thousand miles that year to speak. Eliminated in May from the Lions Club's "Youth of the Year Quest" in Brisbane, he then triumphed in the Jaycees' "Youth Speaks for Australia" competition, winning watches, sets of encyclopaedias, a pile of books on ancient history for the school library and praise from the *Chronicle*: "Once again it's well done Kevin." After the local finals in tiny Biloela and the state finals at Clifton, he flew over to Perth a few weeks after his seventeenth birthday and lost. How did he respond to defeat? "He'd studied Caesar's troubles in the Gallic wars," says Fae Barber laconically. "It stood him in good stead."

What was he going to do once he triumphed – an outcome rightly taken for granted – in his final exams? Perhaps the stage: he had become a keen young actor and the vice-president of Beryl Muspratt's Young People's Theatre of Nambour. In his last year at school he was cast as rather pompous grown-ups in two or three shows, including *Salad Days*, in which he played the Minister of Pleasures and Pastimes, the nark who tries to shut down the magic piano. He learnt everyone's part. Acting and mimicry are Rudd's uncelebrated talents. But he knew he wasn't good enough to go on the stage. The idea was easily and early rejected.

Perhaps the law: so entirely had he immersed himself in the study of *A Man for All Seasons* – Robert Bolt's morality play about the martyrdom of Sir Thomas More at the hands of Henry VIII – that he thought he might become a lawyer and was accepted by the Law School of the University of Queensland. This was not an option he rejected out of hand.

Perhaps diplomacy: towards the end of this cocky kid's time at school, he wrote asking Whitlam how he might become a diplomat. In a reply signed by the man himself – "I held it up to the light each morning to make sure of that" – Whitlam recommended he go to university and study foreign languages. Rudd's mother found the letter. "Consternation broke out in the household … the thought of her son receiving correspondence from Australia's Socialist-in-Chief was a little too much to bear."

Perhaps politics: as early as his final year at school, Rudd began to have glimmerings of political ambition. In these heady years, young Australians fell in love with Labor because Whitlam promised to renew their nation's stale society. Young Rudd's infatuation had another cause. He saw Labor as a gateway to the world: the party that sustained Callander on his foreign adventures and allowed Whitlam his triumphs in China. The boy's political ambitions were vague, indeed barely formed, but they lay beneath all the others. He would have to be something else first and see what political opportunities opened up to him.

He ended 1974 the Dux of Nambour High but decided to postpone university for a year to consider his options. He was only just seventeen. Some months passed before he left town. He worked for a while at Bartholomew's Music Centre on the corner of Queen and Howard streets teaching piano and organ. He toured with Muspratt's company to a students' festival of creative arts and sciences in Canberra. Not perhaps until mid-1975 did he put Nambour behind him and head first to Brisbane – sorting books in the university library and pulling beers at the Paddington Hotel – and then to Sydney. He lived in share houses and grew his blond hair long. If he drank, it was only a little. Drugs were not part of this journey. He told Julia Baird: "I used to have very conservative views about that sort of stuff."

He had spent that last year at school as a swaggering atheist. It hadn't proved convincing. His gap year was a time of religious introspection. He hung round Sydney's Protestant churches hoping to come to a clearer view of Christianity. There he found a faith even less sectarian and less submissive to priests than his mother's. The existence of God was central; the importance of denominations marginal. He could not countenance Papal infallibility nor accept the magisterium of the church, the binding authority of the bishops to teach. The result was a very Rudd compromise reached, perhaps, to cause the least pain all round: he would neither break with Rome nor accept its discipline. He would worship where it suited him. That meant the Uniting Church. He said: "Through that process I came to an adult view of faith."

The last months of 1975 were one of the most turbulent political periods in the history of the country, but young Rudd was taking no part in Labor's struggle. Nor was he galvanised into political activity by turning eighteen and knowing the next election would see him cast his first vote. He was at work on 11 November when he heard Whitlam had been sacked: "I was mopping a floor in the emergency department of the Canterbury Hospital in Sydney where I was employed as a wards man, and I leant on my mop and said: 'That ... is ... mind-boggling.'" Then you picked up the mop? "Oh well, I was on duty."

By year's end he had decided he wasn't a lawyer, wasn't an atheist and wanted – at least for now – to be a diplomat. The boy Frankenstein of Nambour planned yet another transformation of himself: he would make his way towards that career by studying Chinese. Why Chinese, he was asked years later by the ABC journalist Catherine McGrath. Without hesitation he replied: "To escape."

Rudd is lucky. He works at his luck and knows how to use it, but the raw luck of the man at nearly every stage of his life is astonishing. In his first couple of days at the Australian National University's Burgmann College he found Thérèse Rein. She told the *Women's Weekly*:

> We met at a Christian friendship meeting and we started talking on the way back from this meeting. We sat down and had a chat for about an hour and a half, and I liked him. I liked his humour, self-deprecating humour, I liked his integrity, I liked his heart, his compassion if you like, and he's very bright.

She told him: "I think you're the first Kevin I've ever met." He thought the remark "marvellously snotty." The girl was way out of his league: a private-school child from Victoria, daughter of an aeronautical engineer, Anglican. They had important things in common. She too was reaching a resolution about her own beliefs: "I personally committed to Christ." They both knew something of suffering. She told him about her paraplegic father who worked all his life as an engineer while confined to a wheelchair. He confided to her stories the public wouldn't hear for another twenty-five years: "He told me about growing up in Eumundi, losing his father, leaving the farm, his mum training as a nurse, and I thought, he's known suffering in his childhood too." And they talked politics. Rein told Kate Legge of the *Australian*:

> He dissected the fledgling Fraser government, laying forth his vision for the future. "And I said to him, 'Well, I think you should go into federal parliament. I think the nation needs people like you.'"

They fought over many big issues in their years at university, but there was no difference over this: he would one day go into politics. Rein told his biographer Robert Macklin that she waited for this, "From the very first meeting."

Rudd is aware there is a pattern here: a young man who has lost his father as a child setting out to become a political leader. He's done a little reading about this phenomenon, without delving deeply into the lessons it might hold: "I'm not good at reflective questions." Churchill, Eden, Callaghan and Blair are only the latest names on the long list of British prime ministers who were young when their fathers died. Recent names from the American list are Clinton and Obama. The pattern is not so clear in Australia but, counting those whose fathers were for some reason unable to be fathers, we have Andrew Fisher (father incapacitated), Joseph Cook (dead), Joe Lyons (useless), Earle Page (ruined), Ben Chifley (estranged) and poor Billy McMahon, whose mother and father had both shuffled off by the time he was eighteen.

The BBC journalist Jeremy Paxman has drawn on a number of studies to examine what these leaders often have in common:

> A childhood deprived of affection, unusual sensitivity, an outstanding mentor, extreme self-discipline, an overdeveloped religious sense, aggression and timidity, overdependence on the love of others, all featured in many of their lives.

That fits Rudd not quite like a glove, but well enough. He would be more a loner than the pattern suggests. Once he was clear of school and university he would have no mentors other than his mother and his wife. But the rest is there in some measure: the energy, the astonishing emotional resilience Paxman also notes, and the suggestion that he, like other leaders with such dislocated childhoods, sought to patch himself together by pursuing power.

Rudd found power at the university in another quarter altogether. He led a group of evangelicals called the Navigators, intent – or so it seemed to other students – on imposing a puritan rule on Burgmann, a campus college. The Navigators were particularly worried about liquor – Rudd is remembered as a serial complainer about booze being sold in the college bar – rock music and fornication. Philip Hurst, an international lawyer who was then a fellow student at Burgmann, remembers Fresher Rudd vividly: "He would walk down the corridor and in his wake like ducklings after a mother duck were his Christian acolytes." Hurst adds: "It was simply power."

Rudd didn't lift a finger for Labor in the high political excitement of Malcolm Fraser's early years. He didn't march in the streets against Whitlam's nemesis, the governor-general Sir John Kerr, or man the booths in the election campaigns of 1977 and 1980. The wild politics of the campus held no fascination for him. He told me:

> I just thought university politics was a bit silly, to be quite honest. It didn't strike me as being really about real things and I went to university to study and to learn things. I read the student newspaper and read what they were fighting about. It shocked me that they were fighting about castles in the air as opposed to real things. So it never really captured my imagination.

Instead he studied Chinese. His homework was impeccable. He always asked the pertinent question. Fellow students remember him as painfully correct, a bit of a sociopath, almost invisible. But his tutor Pierre Ryckmans (nom de plume: Simon Leys) thought young Rudd a cut above his fellows. "His courtesy, articulateness, impeccable manners and cleanliness (in contrast to the more bohemian and shabby looks of most of his classmates and of his teacher!) always made me assume he came from a rather privileged background, private schools etc.," he told the *Australian Financial Review*'s Lenore Taylor. Rudd spent his fourth year working on the language in Taiwan and returned to ANU to write what was then thought a rather eccentric thesis on the mainland human-rights dissident Wei Jingsheng.

His first-class honours degree opened the door to the Department of Foreign Affairs in January 1981. Later that year, as they were about to leave for a first posting in Stockholm, Rudd and Rein married. She was twenty-three and he was twenty-four. The wedding was in St John's, the old church near the War Memorial where Canberra's powerful pray. Rudd had signed up with his wife's elastic Establishment Anglican flock.

And at last he joined the Labor Party. He was driven to this by fresh hopes, old principles and his new career. His hopes had been stirred by the 1980 election. "Between my Chinese-language classes sitting out there in the student quadrangle in college … I seem to remember the poll indicated that Bill Hayden might actually just get there." Labor clawed back seats but fell far short of victory. But now Rudd felt it was important to take a stand.

> We'd been illegitimately tossed out of office, I was now out of university and now into a working life and my principles on this had not changed and so I decided to formally align …
>
> I was, at that stage, principally taken by Australia's place in the region and in the world. It struck me as a vastly changing world in the frankly post-domino era of south-east and east Asia. Remember

1981 is only six years after the fall of Saigon. So you're looking therefore at a whole new unfolding world ...

Was he thinking of a future political career when he took this step? "As a possibility, yes. As any sort of formal resolution, no."

SUGAR COUNTRY

The land is green, the sea is blue. Coal ships are strung along the horizon. But on this brief hop from Townsville to Mackay only the security guards are gazing out the window. Everyone else on the prime minister's plane has his or her head stuck in a ring binder. Rudd's toy-town version of America's mighty *Air Force One* is a neat jet emblazoned with the familiar but incongruous word *Royal*. As a concession to the needs, or perhaps the addictions, of his staff, mobile phones are only turned off at the very last minute, almost as the plane is leaving the ground. These young men and women look oddly naked without phones to their ears. And they *are* young: in their twenties and early thirties. The work never stops. There is no chiacking. Serving the prime minister may offer them profound satisfaction, but you don't read it on their faces. They make a sombre band.

Rudd was up north handing out large licks of money to hospitals a week or so before his showdown with the premiers in April. His daily routine was this: give early morning radio interviews by phone, visit hospital, give news conference, disappear with staff to attend to matters of state, emerge for coffee or sandwich with local newspaper editors, then fly to next town. Cameras and press trail after him. Everywhere he goes, citizens ask to have their photographs taken with him. Usually one of the security guards takes the snap. Whatever dark techniques they have been taught to protect Rudd's life remain, thank God, a secret. What we did see everywhere on display in North Queensland was their skill with cameras: digital, disposable, SLR and phone.

"They can't be *too* sick," an administrator at the Townsville Hospital confided. Patients the prime minister visits have to be up for the ride, presentable and not at death's door. After all, the footage is destined for the evening news. Yet finding four television cameras, half-a-dozen local journalists, two or three hospital administrators and Kevin Rudd at your bedside is an alarming experience. He asks chipper questions about the disease/condition/operation being endured. He's personable. Not insincere. Then he launches into a little stump speech: "We're here to deliver … seventy million bucks. It's a big investment, but I think it's worth it … It's not just here – we're rolling it out across the country …"

Half an hour later we're in the air. Trim air-force stewards, their hair in neat buns, serve chicken and avocado baguettes with a refreshing glass of water. Rudd wanders out of his room for a cake cutting: one of his staff is leaving after a couple of years on the trail. The celebrations are modest. Rudd is pale, precise and a little puffy. His hair is ghost grey and his eyes are sharp. Standing in the cabin eating a tiny slice of chocolate cake, he has the slightly distracted air of someone who has woken from an afternoon nap. We fall into conversation: about his school days, the Callanders and his time as the right-hand man to Wayne Goss. Did I realise, he asks, that we'd just flown over Mundingburra?

That was the seat in Townsville's suburbs that brought Goss down, a sad end to an extraordinary era. Goss had broken the Nationals' grip on Queensland, come to power with such high hopes and won a second big victory at the polls before his government was carried off on a tide of disappointment, antagonism and weariness. Rudd was at Goss's side almost from beginning to end. There are veterans of the administration who claim Rudd must take a share of the blame for the Goss collapse. They are not without admiration for Rudd's achievements but remember him as an arsehole, mechanical, cold, a cunt, unbelievably arrogant and an absolute prick to deal with. Watch out, they say, history is repeating itself. What happened in Brisbane then is happening in Canberra now.

Rudd's brief diplomatic career had taken him to Beijing after Stockholm. In both posts he impressed his superiors enormously. They gave top marks to this earnest, clever, hard-working man with an urgent need to get things done. He was deft with the powerful people around him, working to be seen by them in a positive light. They thought him a decent man. At this level – Rudd was first secretary in China – diplomacy is not about policy but process. He was very good at process. His mastery of the language was exemplary. Beijing did not leave him with a sentimental affection for China. He was wary and would grow more so as China rose to power once more in the affairs of the world.

Though marked for big things in the department, he seemed a little impatient when he returned to Australia in 1986. His thirtieth birthday found him sitting at a desk in Canberra. By this time, the Rudds had two children: Jessica and Nicholas. It's often said that Rudd is a man always looking to move on. The department had begun to offer diplomats "leave in the public interest" to work with business and political leaders. The short-lived scheme was rather a disaster: no one ever came back. In 1988, Rudd was given a year's leave to be chief of staff to the new leader of the Opposition in Queensland, Wayne Goss. The two men were peas in a pod. They hit it off at their first meeting.

People round Goss were a little taken aback when Rudd appeared in Brisbane in the winter of 1988. "He was bright," says a Labor figure who worked in Rudd's orbit for the next seven years. "But he was nerdy and out of his comfort zone dealing with the sort of personalities you deal with every day in politics. He appeared to have no experience of them at all. But he worked hard at fitting in. We began to hear him cultivating ockerisms. He started to swear in conversation or when he was arguing a point. He wanted to be part of the mob."

Rudd had little impact at first. Directing the overall campaign to restore Labor to government was Wayne Swan, thirty-eight, academic, writer, federal Labor staffer and a former head prefect of Nambour High. He'd been three years ahead of Rudd. They'd not known each other at school. In everyone's mind except Rudd's, Swan was the next generation's Queenslander most likely to succeed in federal politics.

"I identified the top forty companies in Queensland and I obtained their annual reports," Rudd told Lenore Taylor. "I identified their CEOs and directors and I tracked them down. I organised meetings between myself and Wayne [Goss] and all of those people, as well as with all the peak industry bodies in the state." This much-celebrated tactic was straight out of the diplomatic textbook, one he would use time and again in his climb to power. "You need access to operate," the veteran diplomat Richard Woolcott told me. "Good access means you can operate well. If they play chess, you play chess. If they play tennis, play tennis." Rudd, as it happens, plays neither.

The Goss victory in December 1989 ended thirty-two years of National Party government in Queensland. Labor had a sweeping mandate for change, but Goss intended moving cautiously. He told Craig McGregor he had two objectives: "First, to run a traditional Labor government and drive important reforms; and second, to deliver a long-term, stable government. Taking the public with us." His aim was to entrench Labor as the natural government of Queensland. "The last thing we want to be is working-class heroes for three years and mugs for the rest of our lives."

Goss and Rudd drew close. Some say they played to each other's weaknesses. Both are intelligent, driven, cautious and rigorous. Both made heavy demands on their staff. Both cut ill-prepared advisers to shreds. Yet Goss earned the loyalty of those working for him. Rudd didn't. "He was Goss without the humanity," says one of the inner circle. Camaraderie is not his style. He doesn't have the great leader's ability to know when to put the kind hand on the shoulder. But the clarity and energy he brought to government after years of sloth and confusion under Bjelke-Petersen were a revelation. In the middle of 1990 Goss rang Woolcott to ask that Rudd's leave be extended. The premier said: "I've become rather dependent on him."

Rudd became the pre-eminent figure in the government machine the following winter, when Goss set up a Cabinet Office with him at its head. Though designed to work as similar offices did in New South Wales and Victoria – screening submissions from ministers as they moved through to the Cabinet – Rudd had other ideas. As he now boasts in his official CV, he saw himself "driving the Government's reform program as Director General of the Cabinet Office, the central policy agency of the Queensland Government." Hitherto, everyone had passed his desk on the way into

Goss's office. Now he cut a door from his new office into the premier's room so he could still keep an eye on things. One of his colleagues from the time says, "We used to call it the cat-flap."

From this point the accusations began that Rudd was usurping the role of ministers and their departments. His staff of bright young advisers grew from about half-a-dozen until over eighty of them occupied two storeys on George Street. One of those kids for a time was Noel Pearson, co-opted from his legal studies in 1991 to work on the land-rights legislation Rudd had taken out of the hands of the minister for Aboriginal affairs, Anne Warner. Rudd was Pearson's first real boss:

> Notwithstanding the acrimony of our parting … it was not possible to work with Rudd without being impressed by him. I detested what I considered to be his mealy political trimming when dealing with issues that had been on Labor's policy platform during the long winter of National rule in Queensland. But even in the depths of my detestation, I have never been able to deny a grudging regard for Rudd. After all the expletives and bile would come: "Yes, but this man is formidable."

Pearson also remembers him as a daring negotiator. "I recall witnessing a 33-year-old Rudd deal with industry and civic leaders and lobbyists with breathtaking verve and skill." He did have some foibles which old hands noticed early on. He loved to keep people waiting. He was too keen to show he knew more than anyone else in the room about whatever was on the table. Often he did. Deft argument wasn't his only weapon. "You would find to your horror that your secretary has booked him in for an hour to discuss the teaching of Mandarin in high schools," recalls one interstate official. "It's the fifth time you've seen him on the subject. He's absolutely dogged. He gains results by persistence and erosion, by wearing you down."

Rudd had never managed anything in his life. However hard he worked – and he never ceased working – there was an element of chaos and frustration about his office. Material poured in, but not much came out the other end. Rudd's ambition to micro-manage change exceeded his capacity and that of his army of young advisers. Toes were trodden on, noses put out of joint. Public servants were bullied and harassed for information because the office wasn't coping. That aggression was passed down the line. Few had the guts to challenge him. Good work emerged from the Cabinet Office, but it was always hard-won. "The arteries of government were clogged," one old Goss staffer told me. "This was a good system with some very good people, but it was built around a single choke point: Rudd."

Sometime in 1992, Kevin Rudd was seen hanging round the branches in the seat of Griffith. Though it was held by one of Keating's Cabinet ministers, Ben "Gentleman" Humphreys, contenders were already manoeuvring for the succession, which was thought to be a couple of elections away. At this time there was in the air an idea that the successful Goss team might transfer en bloc to Canberra. Swan had pre-selection for the seat of Lilley, north of the river. But it came as a surprise — particularly to the Left faction of the party — that Rudd had his eye on the old waterfront seat of Griffith to the south.

That stretch of the city has had its ups and downs. Traditionally, it took in David Malouf's childhood stamping ground of South Brisbane:

> Edmondstone Street even then was "mixed." Beginning at Melbourne Street, not far from the Bridge, and skirting the south side of Musgrave Park — a dark, uneven place, once an aboriginal burial ground but later redeemed and laid out with Moreton Bay figs of enormous girth and a twelve-foot checker board — it consisted chiefly of old-fashioned, many-roomed houses from the days when this was the most fashionable area south of the river; but there were factories as well …

Rudd had known some of this territory from his childhood: the Mater Hospital was in Griffith. Beyond the hospital were prosperous Liberal suburbs. Labor's strength lay along the river, where the branches were dominated by a small faction known officially as Labor Unity and derisively as the Old Guard. Humphreys was Old Guard through and through. Rudd joined the faction to win the seat, even though it placed him way to the Right of the party and at odds with the dominant AWU faction of the Goss government. He still faced the prospect of a bruising battle to be the party's candidate until 1994, when a redistribution so depleted the Left's forces in Griffith that Rudd became, without rough and tumble, the heir apparent. In October that year Alan Ramsey wrote: "That was all quietly fixed a long time ago."

Rudd's purpose was to become prime minister. Right from the start it was only ever about that. He stood down from his old job and became a mere adviser on commonwealth–state relations in the Office of Cabinet. But he was still part of the inner circle preparing for the state elections in July 1995. Goss seemed assured of victory until a few months from the ballot, when support began to melt away. The polls dipped. Focus groups turned feral: talk of protest votes gave way to talk of booting Goss out. A tetchy campaign saw the government lose nine seats but cling on – for the time being at least – with the help of a single independent.

What had gone wrong? The Right swore Goss had done too much, the Left too little. The Right blamed change fatigue. The Left argued the Goss crowd – and Rudd in particular – had disappointed the high hopes of those who swept Labor to power. Craig McGregor wrote: "On the fateful night in 1989 when Labor at last won government in Queensland, and the relics of Bjelke-Petersen's regime were swept away, Goss told his ecstatic supporters: 'Take a cold shower.' In a way, they've been taking it ever since."

Bad mistakes had been made. Rudd wasn't responsible for the most damaging of them: the decision to renege on old assurances and build a tollway to the Gold Coast. That alone cost Goss five seats. Rudd was remembered for shutting down government services – so many of them so wasteful – in little regional towns. And he had made a particular contribution to the disaffection of the Queensland public service, which had come to loathe all the government stood for. By the time of the poll, Goss had lost the teachers, the nurses, the bureaucrats and the regions. Rudd also had a part in the government's underlying problems of style: the perception out there that Goss and his team always knew best.

Rudd says he has no regrets for the control he exercised, the time he took, the enemies he made, the bureaucrats he frustrated, the staffers he exhausted. He told me: "I know of nobody who's ever occupied a position – either being the chief of staff or a head of a central agency in the public service, state or federal, in this jurisdiction or abroad – who doesn't have those sorts of criticisms levelled at them." That's leadership. Wreckage is to be expected. People are upset when their advice is rejected, their performance criticised, their hopes thwarted. There are no lessons for his career to be drawn from these criticisms. "They are structural to any person who occupies those positions. I say that, by the way, with no sort of idealistic view of any sort of perfection of my role in times past."

Though Rudd sloughs off criticism of his bureaucratic style, he is extremely sensitive to accusations that the policies he was driving were without heart. As he sees it, Goss was preoccupied with the big structural changes necessary to clean up the mess left by the Nationals. That was the principal task of the government's first term. To that end Rudd was deeply involved in ending National Party boondoggles across the state: shutting railways, schools, government offices and hospitals. This policy was deeply resented – not least by the Left of the Labor Party – and would be counted against him in time. Rudd claims he was also pursuing policies to make Queensland a more decent place. The aim was to turn Louisiana into California, but cautiously. Rudd's mantra was: all policy must be evidence-based. But how good were his political instincts? Nil, according to one colleague from those years: "He has a computer-like mind that can analyse all 12,000 policy options, but he chooses by comparing and contrasting, by elimination. Not by instinct." He remains in awe of the way Rudd taught himself to be a formidable bureaucrat but puzzles over his lack of feel. "Does that instinct come from liking and trusting people?" he wonders. "He doesn't have that."

Another of the puzzling aspects of Rudd's years with Goss was his reluctance to put powerful forces offside. He is remembered as a little too willing to take backward steps, too slow to call the bluff of interests long used to getting their way and, in particular, too easily intimidated by business. Perhaps this was almost inevitable in a government of men and women who had grown up in the monoculture of the Bjelke-Petersen era. From the safety of another state, one of Labor's emeritus leaders wonders if there is something particularly Queensland about Rudd: a fugitive sense that the other side is legitimate and Labor the interlopers?

Rudd's blond, serious head was now appearing at the flyscreen doors of Griffith. The thought of this nerd trying to win the hearts and minds of the electorate provoked mirth in party ranks. Not for the last time, he was underestimated. At the age of thirty-eight, Rudd set out to conquer a new skill: campaigning. He did so with all his endless energy and mastery of detail. He taught himself the task almost perfectly. But there was no disguising the fact that he was a most unusual candidate. At a roast and fundraiser at Brisbane's Sheraton Hotel – the cream of Rudd's contact book was there and CUB donated the booze – the deputy prime minister, Kim Beazley, told a little story. When Gareth Evans was elected to the Senate, his colleagues at Melbourne University gave him, said Beazley, a couple of suitcases to carry his ego to Canberra. "You might like to think about that, Kevin."

Perhaps what happened next was karma. Complaints about the conduct of the poll in the state seat of Mundingburra led first to an inquiry and then to a by-election. Opinion polls had Labor heading for a narrow victory there until Paul Keating called the 1996 federal election. Mundingburra was lost. A few days later, Goss finally folded.

Rudd's own situation was precarious. The redistribution that delivered him federal pre-selection made Griffith much harder for Labor to hold. And as Goss said: "Queenslanders are sitting on their verandas with baseball bats just waiting for Keating to come." Thérèse Rein joined her husband on the beat. The Rudds rallied from Nambour. By polling day in March 1996, they had knocked on most of the 32,000 doors of Holland Park, Norman Park, Coorparoo, Gumdale, Tingalpa, Camp Hill, Balmoral, Morningside, Hawthorne and Bulimba. But it didn't work. Eleven of Labor's thirteen seats in Queensland were wiped out. Swan lost Lilley. Pauline Hanson won Oxley. Rudd didn't win Griffith. Keating lost government.

Rudd was shattered. The hostility of his electorate could be measured with pinpoint accuracy. He was utterly unused to losing. Out of the wreckage of his childhood had come an extraordinary narrative of success. Everyone's expectations had been exceeded, except his own. Now he had lost. He believes commentators never grasp how terrible this is. It's left him, he says, with deep sympathy even for his opponents when they face the people and lose. Schadenfreude was freely expressed by his critics: they hoped he might now be a little humbler, might start to listen. That appears not to have been the lesson he drew from this engagement with democracy. The secret of Rudd's success has always been his astonishing emotional resilience. He moped and raged for a while after March 1996, then put himself back in harness.

He had no job. He and Rein decided it was time he returned to his old department, in the hierarchy of which he had continued to rise while absent on leave. They were looking for a minister in Beijing and consul-general in Shanghai. His return was in train when Philip Flood, the new secretary Howard appointed to the department, let it be known that Rudd's career had been "too colourful" and that he was to take voluntary redundancy. Rudd knew that he couldn't be sacked in this way but with an old adversary, Alexander Downer, now minister, he could see himself languishing forever in obscure posts. He took redundancy and became a freelance adviser to business on dealing with China. His principal client was KPMG.

"He had no trouble working a long day," recalls Stephen Lonie, the then managing partner of the firm in Queensland. "He was intensely driven." Rudd made introductions rather than doing deals. He helped corporations in trouble. His presence wasn't always welcomed. He trod on the toes of the KPMG partners in Hong Kong. But he was rated capable, a success. It was always clear he was going to pursue politics. "The game is on again," he told Lonie sometime in 1998. "I'm getting out the van. If I win, it's over. If I lose, I'll be back again."

He knocked on doors. He railed against aircraft noise and the prospect of John Howard's GST. He and Lindsay Tanner in silly hats rode a tandem bike through the city to promote the Opposition's bicycle policy. The turning political tide saw Labor win back six of its old seats in Queensland and Kim Beazley nearly win office from Howard. Swan regained Lilley. Hanson lost Oxley. Rudd became the member for Griffith and turned up in Canberra in November to take his seat and immediately deliver his maiden speech. His mother was in the gallery.

More often than not, going through the entrails of these speeches is a waste of time. Not so in Rudd's case. Most of what matters in his politics is sketched here:

> When my father was accidentally killed and my mother, like thousands of others, was left to rely on the bleak charity of the time to raise a family, it made a young person think. It made me think that a decent social-security system designed to protect the weak was no bad thing. It made me think that the provision of decent public housing to the poor was the right thing to do. When I saw people unnecessarily die in the appallingly under-funded Queensland hospital system of the 1960s and 1970s, it made me think that the provision of a decent universal health system should be one of the first responsibilities of the state.

The key word is decent. Nothing radical is proposed. The vision is personal and conservative. His ambitions for government were old-fashioned: to pursue the public good at home and abroad. Government must be made a better machine for regulating markets and caring for those who cannot look after themselves. Australia must secure the respect of its neighbours and be active in world forums. Though these appear to be modest aims – a clarion call for fine-tuning – Rudd sees himself on a transformative mission. To think otherwise is to misunderstand him entirely. He won't acknowledge any incongruity between his policy and his political ambitions. Both are big. Perhaps the two can't be disentangled in his mind. The first words of that first speech Rudd gave in parliament were, "Politics is about power."

SUNRISE

Hundreds of us were trapped for two and a half hours without interval in a rowdy piece of community theatre called *Waiting for Kevin*. Everyone was shouting. No one could be heard. Beautiful young party workers – children the last time Canberra changed hands – posed in "Kevin 07" T-shirts. Cameras flashed like firecrackers. Up on the big screens Kerry O'Brien was tolling through the count like an old priest saying mass. No one was listening. A little after 7 p.m. Queensland time, the premier, Anna Bligh, appeared from the party's headquarters upstairs and walked through the melee confiding to those in her path: "Kevin Rudd is the prime minister of Australia."

But there was no sign of Kevin. As the scythe of democracy cut across Australia, the decibels kept rising in that long room under Brisbane's Suncorp Stadium. The rough dignity of John Howard's concession speech was met with cat-calls and booing. Only the sight of Maxine McKew hushed the crowd for a few moments at a time. Her battle for the seat of Bennelong was the nearest the night had to a cliff-hanger. She won, she lost and she seemed to be winning again. Over her left shoulder could be glimpsed the old party strategist Bob Hogg, struggling to hide his triumph as his partner trounced the man who had dominated Australian politics for a dozen years.

Men with wires in their ears appeared from nowhere, generic rock and roll pumped out of the speakers and Rudd was among us, a pale, neatly dressed man with a tight smile. His eyes were invisible. The room responded with a mighty roar as he and his family climbed onto the platform: "Kevin. Kevin. Kevin." Thérèse Rein was ecstatic. The pride of the children in the face of this ovation was heart-stopping. Then Rudd killed the party.

"OK, guys," he said, holding up his hands like a slightly weary teacher to shush the rowdy enthusiasm. "A short time ago, Mr Howard called me to offer his congratulations …" Such courtesies are obligatory, of course, but Rudd went on and on about the virtues of his fallen opponent. The revellers waited him out: waited to burst back into life; waited for the moment when Rudd's face would break into a smile of triumph; waited for him to lead the celebrations. That never happened. The rhetoric was leaden:

> Today Australia has looked to the future. Today the Australian people have decided that we as a nation will move forward to plan for the future, to prepare for the future, to embrace the future and together, as Australians, to unite and write a new page in our nation's history to make this great country of ours, Australia, even greater.

He seemed neither to welcome nor need acclaim. He wasn't basking in the verdict of the ballot box or the delight of his audience. God knows what emotions were coursing through him on the platform – vindication, relief or perhaps exhaustion, after having fought his way towards this moment for at least twenty years – but he was losing the crowd. Rein could tell: her face fell as he ploughed on.

> Tomorrow, and I say this to the team, we roll up our sleeves, we're ready for hard work. We're ready for the long haul. You can have a strong cup of tea if you want in the meantime; even an Iced Vo Vo on the way through, for the celebrations should stop there. We have a job of work to do. It's time, friends, for us, together as a nation, to bind together to write this new page in our great nation's history. I thank the nation.

The klieg lights went out. The cameras packed up. The screens fell silent. That was about it for the party. Sober revellers wandered out into a warm Brisbane night. The peculiarities of the event were passed off as a joke: that's Kevin! But at victory celebrations across the nation there were those who, however jubilant to see the back of Howard, asked themselves: what have we here?

"Leadership," Rudd told me, "is always a lonely race. Anyone honest about their reflections on that reaches the same conclusion." Through hard and lonely work he won the leadership of his party. "I've always just been a person who believes in rowing his own race, that is, doing what you believe to be the right thing, doing it with vigour, doing it with conviction and doing it with determination." True enough. Bob Carr remembers the years, the determination and the work Rudd put into climbing to the top: "He nagged the party into it, kept insisting. He willed himself there. He couldn't be overlooked. He was always in your diary or at your door."

Rudd's arrival in Canberra in 1998 hadn't set caucus alight. He didn't hide his ambitions. "There was only one job he was really interested in, and that was being prime minister," says the Labor strategist Bruce Hawker. To be shooting so high so soon marked him as a bit of a prat. Beazley was no fan. He was not given a place on the front bench. Rudd's position was, indeed, lonely: the Brisbane Old Guard was a faction of two and he made few friends in Labor ranks. Where, they wondered, did he fit?

Mark Latham put him on the list of "more careerists, more technocrats, more plodders" who turned up on the Labor side of parliament at that time. The new man wasn't tribal Labor nor did he revel in Labor history. He didn't join those in the party – mainly from New South Wales – who worship the ground the US Democrats walk on. One of the few political heroes Rudd mentioned in these years was Keir Hardie, the Christian socialist who founded the party in Britain:

> He was a man who thought rolling up to church on Sunday without engaging the resources of the state to improve the lot of his fellow man was a recipe for hypocrisy.

What his puzzled new companions in caucus missed was the peculiarly personal nature of Rudd's political faith: a commitment to politics growing not out of history, work or ideological conviction but out of the public and private hell of his childhood.

With customary zeal, Rudd began networking. He courted journalists and would, in time, cheerfully admit to being a "media tart." He wrote high-falutin' stuff about China for newspapers and worked the press gallery. In the long political silence of the Christmas break, he was infallibly working, travelling, always ready to be interviewed. "This rather strange, isolated will o' the wisp would bob up every now and again, knock on the door and come in," recalls Alan Ramsey. "When you rang him, he was always away. He'd never answer but ring back from somewhere in the world a day or so later." Winter is think-tank season in Australia and Rudd never missed the annual gatherings convened by the Centre for Independent Studies, the Australian American Leadership Dialogue – he had been a member since it began in 1993 – and the Australian Davos Connection. "He would be there from the first drinks to the last lunch, whether contributing to a session or not," remarked a wry fellow-attendee. "He would be there cultivating these business people." Perhaps here is an explanation for 2020, the great conference he called on becoming prime minister. The mass of ideas it generated have got nowhere, but they probably weren't the point: it was an opportunity on a huge scale for Rudd to network.

Another figure would have earned the admiration of caucus for throwing himself so energetically into the business of being known. But something about this man jarred with his colleagues. They thought him too dogged, too cool, too academic. That he had such impossible ambitions made his efforts seem absurd. Once again Rudd was being underestimated. As he had taught himself to be a bureaucrat and a candidate, he would teach himself to be a politician. And he wouldn't trust his future to caucus: he would make his own mark. That's where Channel Seven's *Sunrise* comes into the Rudd story. One of Rudd's former staffers told me: "It was an operation to cook caucus from the outside."

With the muddy Brisbane River over his shoulder, a rather woebegone Rudd appeared on the show for the first time in February 2001. "He needed work," admits Hawker, who knew Rudd from the days of helping on Goss's election campaigns and suggested him to the show's producers. "He did need to become a much more direct communicator." Just as woeful was the sparring partner Rudd produced: his parliamentary prayer-breakfast mate, the Liberal politician Ross Cameron. The show was a dog and the politicians were dull. The future of the whole enterprise was uncertain. Cameron asked his flatmate Joe Hockey to stand in for him once or twice and the producers wanted the cheerful minister for small business to stay. Hockey told me: "Rudd went in a flat panic to Cameron to say that if he didn't make way for me, the segment was going to be lost." Cameron made way. A new producer arrived and David Koch became one of the show's presenters. Hockey and Rudd went on to be "The Big Guns of Politics" for the next six years as *Sunrise* turned into one of the most watched shows on Australian television.

"It was retail politics," says Hockey. "It introduced us to an audience that wasn't interested in politics. The audience loved the fact that we looked like mates. They accepted that Kevin was the straight-laced one on the team. He found on *Sunrise* a constituency that supported him: mums with kids. They liked him. They accepted this terribly careful guy because it was part of the routine. They didn't switch off. They liked us – mums under forty-five with a couple of kids, doing the double drop-off, working a couple of days a week to pay the huge mortgage. The show talked about its target being, I think, Mary from Ipswich. Howard treated these people with indifference and it was a great failing."

The *Tampa* election of 2001 saw Labor lose ground, Rudd increase his majority – the placards in Griffith read "Keep Kevin" – and Kim Beazley relinquish the leadership of the Opposition. The new leader, Simon Crean, tribal Labor to the fingertips, made Rudd the party's spokesman for foreign affairs. He would spend the next five years jousting with his unpromising contemporary in the Department of Foreign Affairs, Alexander Downer. It was always personal.

Crean performed poorly. As the invasion of Iraq loomed, Rudd was left to finesse the policy contradictions of a deeply divided Opposition. It didn't help that his advice to Crean was wrong: Rudd insisted the UN would decide on the invasion and that weapons of mass destruction would be found. As confused as Labor's position was, the debates of 2002 gave Rudd unprecedented public exposure. Television cameras followed him to New York, Jakarta, Zimbabwe and the Afghan border. Labor voted against the war when it came, but many in the party blamed Rudd for Labor's opposition to the war not being sharper, sooner. Crean seemed unlikely to survive.

Even at this early point, Rudd saw himself as a contender. He had essentially no support in caucus and little backing from the public. His name cropped up in Newspolls for the first time in late 2002 and April 2003, but he appeared to be in a hopeless position, with only 4 or 5 per cent naming him as their choice to lead Labor. That put him in the pack with Latham and Swan. This is the moment – after the invasion of Iraq and those early Newspolls, with a challenge to Crean in the air – when Rudd began to flesh out the story of his life for the first time.

On 18 April the *Age* carried Michael Gordon's fine profile of "the stand-out performer on the Crean front bench." It was a mixed blessing. The hostility of caucus to Rudd was vividly presented:

> "It's like he's got a grand flaw," said one who bears him no ill will. "He has all these tremendous attributes … but the flaw is his inability to read how people are reacting to him. His response is to adopt a boss–underling approach, which among equals tends to build resentment."

But the public read – and remembered – Rudd talking of Bert's death, the eviction from Eumundi, something of the turmoil of the years that followed and the nadir reached the night he slept rough in the VW with his sister and mother:

> People ask: how did I end up in the Labor Party, having grown up in a conservative political environment? If I trace it back, I just

remember sleeping in the car that night and thinking, "This is crook. This should not happen to anyone."

Rudd's media assault in 2003 worked beautifully. In a little over six months, support for his candidacy rose fourfold to more than 20 per cent. Maxine McKew gave Rudd a lavish spread in the *Bulletin* that allowed him to display his intellectual charm and leadership potential while reassuring readers about his reputation as a God-botherer. He declared: "I'm a Jeffersonian separatist." McKew remarked that this man had "more votes in the community than in caucus." That, in a nutshell, was the problem Rudd would face for the next hard-fought years. *Sunrise* and the profiles had lifted him out of the ruck. Swan was never a leadership contender after this. The two men who had been sharing a house in Canberra fell out badly. But the higher public profile didn't help Rudd win support where he needed it: in the parliamentary party.

Beazley moved too soon against Crean. At that mid-year attempt, Rudd voted for Beazley but not before letting it be known in the press gallery that he had seriously considered making a run himself. When a besieged Crean eventually decided on 28 November to resign, Rudd considered it his turn. Though pollsters had Beazley as the overwhelming choice of the public to lead the Opposition once more, Rudd was favoured over the only other contender, Mark Latham. A McNair Ingenuity poll in the *Sunday Telegraph* ranked support for the contenders as Beazley 47 per cent, Rudd 24 per cent and Latham 18 per cent. A Morgan poll published days later had the same message of hope for Rudd but slightly different figures: Beazley 38 per cent, Rudd 21 per cent and Latham 17.5 per cent. The pollster found:

> Those who preferred Mr Rudd liked the style of his politics and thought he was a better choice than other potential candidates for the position.
>
> "I like the sound of his politics. Latham's too divisive, Beazley's had his turn, I don't know about Swan."

"Beazley's going backwards. He's already had a go."

"He's young, intelligent, articulate. He handles his portfolio well."

"He speaks well and presents himself well."

"New blood, new ideas."

Yet Rudd could muster only eleven votes in caucus. Had he stood he would have been routed. He never put up his hand. Latham narrowly beat Beazley. A senior Labor figure tried without success to comfort a very unhappy Rudd: "I know you're shattered, but Latham is someone Labor has to get out of its system. If you'd won, he'd be shadowing you. Now it's him. Then he will be out of the way."

From this defeat, Rudd drew the lesson that it was time to court caucus as assiduously as he had been courting the public. So began a three-year campaign to convince his colleagues that he was next in line. Rudd went about this in a way that was typically disciplined and systematic, absolutely appropriate and faintly absurd. Spreadsheets were prepared containing everything that mattered about every one of them, down to their children's names and wives' birthdays. He began to hang about awkwardly in the bars where his colleagues drank. He let them talk. He practised the art of listening. It was camaraderie by numbers. He flew all over the place, popping up unexpectedly at Labor events around the country. "He would be there just to be there," says one party official in Sydney. "At a retirement dinner for a union secretary, Rudd would turn up, not to speak, not to be in the official party, not even to be acknowledged by the chair – but just to be there."

Latham loathed and distrusted the man he called "Heavy Kevvie" and the "King of Caveats." But he should have listened. In March 2004 Latham complained to his diary:

> He sounds incomprehensible in the media whenever he talks about Iraq ... Rudd wanted our policy on the troops to be a review when we got into government. Imagine the pounding we would have taken on such a wishy-washy stance, so I overruled him and said

> yesterday that we wanted them home by Christmas. I've had a firm position on every other issue and it's worked for me; why not this one?

With that, Latham began his long slide in the polls. For months he had been dominating politics, but once he declared Labor's intention to withdraw the troops, he was pounded. Howard was triumphant once more. Labor slouched towards another defeat.

Rudd got on with his ceaseless work. Neither his demands nor his methods appeared to have changed from his Brisbane days, but now, instead of a staff of eighty-plus to call on, he had only two or three. He drove them hard. They came and went. One told me:

> His office is chaotic. He would schedule staff meetings at bizarre times – like 10 p.m. on a Sunday night when parliament is sitting next day. And because he is busy doing other things, the 10 p.m. meeting doesn't start until 1 a.m.
>
> Because everything is on the go at once and he's interrogating the detail of everything, nothing comes out until the last minute. Bringing work to a conclusion was focused around the next media hit. He loves an announcement.
>
> He has an enormous appetite for raw information. He believes if you shake the raw material the answer will fall out all of its own accord. He wants the data. He likes the material organised in matrixes – big spreadsheets showing who knows what when.
>
> He doesn't trust his advisers to give advice, so they become glorified research assistants. The Parliamentary Library was also researching – rather than analysing – for him. He had them tied in knots with every request. They pushed back a few times when the load got too heavy. But he does read everything he asks for.
>
> He is a strange beast behind closed doors. He is so focused on the day-to-day tasks that he loses the social niceties. They are neither here nor there. Staff are interrogated beyond what's reasonable

to expect them to know. And if you don't know, the atmosphere changes. Not a blow-up. It becomes very quiet. But he doesn't deliberately push his staff to this point.

For all the effort, he doesn't come up with particularly interesting solutions to problems. His policy positions aren't breakthroughs, not particularly new or exciting. After all that work they are dull.

It was always hard grind. Even when you had big wins, the mood was: well, what's next?

By this time Rudd had acquired Alister Jordan, a slight, sharp-eyed man dubbed Mr April by the rest of the staff. "There was no reason to expect the 22-year-old who'd answered a newspaper job ad would survive any longer than the others, Mr January and Mr February," explained Phillip Hudson in the *Sydney Morning Herald*. A recent political science graduate from Queensland, Jordan was first office manager, then adviser and finally Rudd's chief of staff. He is still there after working 100 hours a week for the man for nearly ten years. Jordan became part of the Rudd family. He is said to be the only person in politics Rudd trusts.

Marge Rudd died at the age of eighty-three on the day before the country went to the polls in October 2004. The knowledge that he had spent the last days of his mother's life campaigning for a man he could not respect filled Rudd with rage. He judged that Latham was on the skids and that it was time to broaden his own appeal with the party and the public. But Latham refused Rudd the promotion he wanted and bitterly accused him of leaking to the press. In one of the most notorious passages in his diary, Latham wrote:

> He appeared surprised, protested his innocence and then broke down badly, sobbing over the recent death of his mother, just before polling day. Rudd was in a very fragile condition. I told him to leave work and go back to Brisbane to rest with his family. But he wouldn't give up. Even though he was crying, he kept lobbying to be Shadow Treasurer. It was becoming quite sad.

But Latham was the one who had the breakdown. First he retreated with his family and then, goaded to fury by press complaints that he'd failed to respond decently to the Asian tsunami, he called the press to a bleak park in Western Sydney and resigned from public life. Rudd, up in Aceh to inspect the damage and offer bipartisan support for Howard's billion-dollar gift to Indonesia, flew home to canvass support and found Beazley once again blocking his road.

Australians loved Beazley. They might not vote for the Bomber, but they loved to see him leading the Labor Party. The polls of late January 2005 spoke with a single voice: Beazley was the man. Rudd was stuck where he was at the last challenge: in the low 20 per cents. Behind him with a swathe of Latham's votes was a new contender, the left-wing Victorian Julia Gillard. Her public support was in the high teens. Rudd and Jordan spent the weekend of 22 to 23 January canvassing caucus for support. Against Beazley they could muster only seventeen or eighteen votes. His colleagues disdained his bid. Again he threw in the towel. A deal was done at this point: in return for allowing the old leader to be re-elected unopposed, Rudd would be next in line should Beazley fail. Such deals are, of course, notoriously unenforceable.

The party showered Rudd with praise for standing aside. "I've got a field marshal's baton in the backpack," he told the press. "It's just that during the current term of the Australian parliament it's not possible to take that baton out." Beazley wanted to shift him to education. He absolutely refused, for education would take him out of the public eye. Another long haul lay ahead and foreign affairs would keep him in the news all the time. Beazley had no choice. Rudd also insisted that trade be added to his responsibilities. Rudd now had authority to talk across the economy.

Nine months later, Paul Volcker, the former chairman of the US Federal Reserve, revealed that AWB Limited – formerly the Australian Wheat Board – had paid $300 million in kickbacks to the regime of Saddam Hussein. Volcker's investigation of the UN Oil-for-Food Programme had identified AWB as the biggest single source of corrupt payments to Iraq before the invasion. The Howard government, after working hand in glove with AWB for some time to keep a lid on the scandal, was forced to hold a public inquiry into the wheat sales. But the terms of reference given to Terence Cole QC were carefully crafted: he had no authority to delve into the government's role in the affair.

Rudd was made for the attack he sustained on the government for the next year. The rich and complex detail of the story Rudd mastered effortlessly. Few but the lawyers knew the case so well. Once more he had Downer in his sights, for the minister for foreign affairs had signed permits for 292 ships to carry wheat worth over $2 billion to Iraq – and almost every contract was laden with kickbacks that breached UN sanctions. Night after night on television, day after day in parliament Rudd lashed the government for turning a blind eye, failing to heed warnings, lying, covering up, pretending to know nothing and now refusing to allow Cole to investigate Downer and his department: "The terms of reference make it possible for a firing squad to be put together for the Australian Wheat Board while taking the Howard government out of the firing line altogether."

Rudd was painting the prime minister as a habitual liar. Grandees of the Canberra press gallery sneer at the issue – aren't all politicians liars? – but Rudd's attack was highly effective, wounding Howard and simultaneously fashioning his own image as professional and truthful. The big essay on faith he wrote later in 2006 would argue for Christianity as the religion of truth-tellers, indeed of martyrs for the truth. A panegyric for Dietrich Bonhoeffer, "whose political theology is one of a dissenting church that speaks truth to the state," it would end in a magisterial attack on Howard the liar: "The prime minister's now routine manipulation of the truth poses significant problems for the long-term integrity of our national institutions …"

This relentless pursuit of Howard won Rudd the friends he needed in the party. Hawker argues: "The real breakthrough was the wheat scandal. It made him in the eyes of caucus and the powerbrokers." The Christian

Rudd with a passion for diplomacy was not the man they wanted. They were after a fighter, a smart and determined fighter, to defeat John Howard's union-busting WorkChoices. The NSW unions under John "Robbo" Robertson, who had masterminded a brilliant television campaign against the legislation, were becoming impatient with Beazley's failure to gain traction on the issue in Canberra.

Every Friday, Rudd flew to Sydney for *Sunrise*. The show was working better than ever. The "Big Guns of Politics" segment had been moved to the highest-rating slot on the highest-rating day of the week. He and Hockey pulled off a television triumph in 2006 by climbing the Kokoda Track together to celebrate Anzac Day live on *Sunrise*. Rudd would have breakfast with Hockey after the show every Friday and then do his rounds of the town, usually calling at Sussex Street, where early 2006 found him in conversation with Robertson over the party leadership. After backing Beazley through thick and thin – he was on a crash diet at this time to impress the voters – the forces of the NSW Right, the king-makers of Labor, were splintering. Most were ready to switch to Rudd.

Rudd's position was suddenly complicated by Gillard, who in April began overtaking him in the polls. The two had very similar problems. Both had worked hard at building high public profiles, but both were thwarted in caucus: he by distrust and distaste, she by coming from the Left. At no time in living memory had Labor chosen anyone from the Left as its federal leader. That winter, Rudd and Gillard recognised their mutual interest and began to talk. A battle between them would see both wiped out. Yet if they could unite, Beazley was gone for all money. Gillard was ahead of Rudd in both the polls – 31 to 27 per cent – and in the caucus – about twenty-eight votes to his sixteen – but he would not run on her ticket.

On the last Monday of November, Cole's five-volume report on the AWB scandal was tabled in parliament. It may have been as late as that week that Rudd and Gillard finally settled their pact. They deny a Kirribilli clause governing the succession. She was taking her chances: if they failed to win the next election, it would be her turn after that. Bob Hawke rang to say Beazley should be left alone. Rudd says he replied: "Get fucked." He asked the NSW Left MP Anthony Albanese to stand in for him that Friday on *Sunrise*. Rein said "Go for it," and he walked down the corridor and told Beazley the fight was on.

The execution had been exquisitely choreographed. The press was in the dark. As Rudd returned from Beazley's rooms, the first Labor member rang a designated journalist at AAP to say she was supporting Kevin Rudd's challenge called that morning. His supporters continued ringing AAP through the day. Jordan and Rudd were confident they could win but not sure of having the convincing victory they needed. Caucus loved Beazley, not the challenger. Though the three-year charm offensive had warmed a few hearts, Rudd still had not many friends and no solid faction. But over the weekend the party professionals moved in behind him. Old enemies were canvassing on the contender's behalf. Labor had to come out of this bloodletting looking as if it had finally made up its mind. And no one in caucus doubted Rudd's determination. "I've seen some driven politicians in my time, but I have seen no one more driven than Kevin," Senator John Faulkner told me. "But this is a good thing, not a bad thing. It's what the Labor Party needed after that long period of Liberal government. You have to be driven to succeed. You have to be driven to overcome the advantages of incumbency."

On Monday, 4 December 2006, Beazley lost to Rudd thirty-nine votes to forty-nine. Howard's strategist and pollster Mark Textor was not happy: "As a professional of fifteen or twenty years' standing, I was deeply worried almost immediately after the leadership change." Rudd would prove the party's most potent electoral machine since Bob Hawke, but this was not clear at first. Beazley already had Labor well ahead in the polls, but similar leads had disappeared as he campaigned in 1998 and 2001. Latham had been way ahead of the government in 2004, but that lead had evaporated too. The challenge for Rudd was to hold Labor's lead all the way to the ballot box. One advantage over Beazley lay deep down in the figures: Rudd would magically restore the party's primary vote. He straddled a vast political divide: Greens on the Left and Christians on the Right would give their first vote to Labor under him. Also clear in a Newspoll published on the morning of his caucus victory was the public's enthusiasm for the Rudd/Gillard team (52 per cent support) and weariness with the old Beazley/Macklin leadership (27 per cent support). But the voters continued to admire the prime minister as a *person*. On none of the usual measures – e.g. "decisive and strong," "in touch with the voters," "has a vision for Australia" – did the change of leaders trump Howard.

Then Australia saw Rudd in action. In the media blitz of those first days, he returned to the themes he had brought with him into politics: compassion, fairness and decency. There was clunky talk of forks in the road and bridges too far, but what caught the national imagination at this low point in our politics was a fresh, young, smiling leader backing simple, old virtues. The man the party chose for his fighting qualities was embraced by the public for promising to bring sweetness and light to politics. Addressing parliament as leader of the Opposition for the first time, Rudd gave one of the most eloquent performances of his career, delivering, essentially, his maiden speech all over again:

> Compassion is not a dirty word. Compassion is not a sign of weakness. In my view, compassion in politics and in public policy is in fact a hallmark of great strength. It is a hallmark of a society which has about it a decency which speaks for itself. For us in the Labor movement from which we proudly come and have come this last century, these values of security, liberty and opportunity are not incompatible with equity, with sustainability and with compassion ...
>
> So the battlelines are drawn in this great battle of ideas between us. In the ten days or so ahead, when we leave this place, I will be travelling the country, taking this message out. This is not just a battle for ideas; it is a battle on the ground as well. I say to those

opposite: we intend to prevail in this battle of ideas, on the ground, right through to the next election. We intend to prevail.

He did. The more Australians saw him, the more they liked him. Petty scandals were brushed aside. Drinks at a strip club, covert contact with a Labor bagman, the row with the Lows over the Eumundi eviction, calling dawn early on Anzac Day for the convenience of *Sunrise* – that saw the end of the "Big Guns" – rumours of a filthy temper and news that his heart had been patched up left his popularity untouched. Indeed, he emerged from these tabloid smears a little stronger each time. From early 2007 he was the most popular Opposition leader since polling began in Australia.

That summer he took a camera crew to Eumundi and shot a commercial that went to air on Australia Day. It was masterful: back home had come the boy once desperate to escape, now a politician claiming his due as a son of the land. The text was superior boilerplate: stuff about Mum and Dad, education, a strong economy and a fair go. But tucked in there was something Rudd really believed in, something his return to Eumundi proved true: "Some call us the lucky country, but I believe you make your own luck."

The polls showed Australians wanted Rudd to be prime minister and Labor's two-party-preferred vote threatened the government with something like annihilation. The man caucus had regarded for so long as a try-hard chameleon was thought far more trustworthy (67 to 49 per cent), far more in touch with voters (76 to 50 per cent) and much more likeable (82 to 55 per cent) than the prime minister. Howard was not despised. A Nielsen poll in June showed voters still thought him the better man to handle the economy and even foreign policy. But young Rudd was thought way ahead of old Howard in his grasp of social policy (68 to 43 per cent), understanding of climate change (71 to 37 per cent) and overall public approval (63 to 50 per cent). This was a man who could do superbly what all who crave high office must do: harvest a nation's hopes.

Yet all the way to victory night at the Suncorp Stadium there was a question in the air: can Australia have a leader who's an ash-blond, unfit, smiling nerd? The answer that night was yes. Nerd leaders are fine by Australians. We like experts. We like ideas. We value competence in our leaders. We choose them much as we choose an electrician: because they can be trusted to get on with their complicated work. We have a long tradition of electing such leaders. The campaign of 2007 was a face-off between two nerds: eleven years of power hadn't altogether disguised the gawky, opportunistic policy wonk that was John Howard. As the polling analyst Andrew Catsaras told me: "The Paul Hogan era is over. Australians want their leaders to be competent, intelligent and able to do the job."

Rudd was sworn in at Yarralumla on 3 December 2007. The Queen's name did not pass his lips. Instead of allegiance he swore to "well and truly serve the Commonwealth of Australia, her land and her people, so help me God." On his first day in office, he signed the Kyoto Protocol. On the first day of parliament he delivered an apology to the stolen generations into which he threw what was most authentic about his politics: his instinctive sympathy for children and for the survivors of wretched childhoods. His coarse – but popular – intervention in the controversy over Bill Henson's photographs the following May flowed from the same source. "Absolutely revolting," he declared after a few seconds' scrutiny of redacted images on a television monitor. "Kids deserve to have the innocence of their childhood protected. I have a very deep view of this. For God's sake, let's just allow kids to be kids." Hovering over his attack on Henson as much as the extraordinarily fine Apology are the ghosts of Eumundi and Ashgrove.

The Apology had not come easily. Having trouble drafting his speech, Rudd went to see Lorna Fejo, who had come down from the Territory for the occasion. Fejo had been ripped out of her mother's arms by white police and a black stockman in a bush camp in Tennant Creek in the 1930s:

I asked Nanna Fejo what she would have me say today about her story. She thought for a few moments then said that what I should say today was that all mothers are important. And she added: "Families – keeping them together is very important. It's a good thing that you are surrounded by love and that love is passed down the generations. That's what gives you happiness." As I left, later on, Nanna Fejo took one of my staff aside, wanting to make sure that I was not too hard on the Aboriginal stockman who had hunted those kids down all those years ago. The stockman had found her again decades later, this time himself to say, "Sorry." And remarkably, extraordinarily, she had forgiven him.

It was a great day for tears. Inside the house, on the lawns of parliament, in squares and streets across Australia, crowds were weeping, more with relief than anything that the country's sorry business had finally been done. On his first day in parliament the new prime minister walked into the history books. It seemed we had elected a man of principle and courage.

MAN FOR ALL SEASONS

Shriven, blameless, fresh from communion, the prime minister stands at the lych-gate of St John's Canberra and takes questions from the media. Although he rarely does the rounds of the Sunday morning current-affairs shows, Rudd stands at the gate of the old church on Constitution Avenue, available for the cameras, whenever Sunday finds him in Canberra. The message is clear: this prime minister mixes faith and politics. It makes Rudd an odd man out among Labor prime ministers. The last keen believer to lead a Labor government was Scullin. Not since the Second World War has Australia had a self-confessed God-botherer of any political persuasion running the country. The sight of a prime minister using a church as backdrop for a press conference sets many Australians on edge. But it's authentic Rudd and he knows it plays surprisingly well to the electorate.

Who is Rudd? A political Christian. After Labor's defeat in October 2004, Rudd took command of an operation to win believers back to the party. A strong religious undertow had worked against Labor in the campaign. Atheist Mark Latham with plans to cut the cash flowing to rich church schools was pitted against John Howard the prince of Family Values. Howard was employing some of the tricks and rhetoric sweeping George W. Bush to a second victory in those same weeks in the US. A shrewd deal to swap preferences with Family First, a party set up by the Assemblies of God, put Steve Fielding into the Senate and on Rudd's analysis cost Labor at least four marginal seats. A month after the poll Rudd declared on Channel Ten:

> We will not for one moment stand idly by while either the Liberals, Nationals or Family First assert that God has somehow become some wholly owned subsidiary of political conservatism in this country.

The fight to reclaim Christ for Labor began with a PowerPoint presentation in Rudd's parliamentary office in late November. Spilling from his room into the hallway was nearly a third of the caucus: believers and non-believers from all factions. What they planned was unfamiliar work, but if winning meant grappling with God, then it had to be done. Rudd found an ally in Jim Wallis, a visiting American preacher who was out here to promote his book *God's Politics*. Wallis was to become a key figure in the claw-back of Christian votes by US Democrats. The operations in America and Australia moved roughly in parallel. The two men kept in touch.

Rudd was appealing to a bigger audience than the 8 per cent of Australians who join him in prayer on any given Sunday. Australia remains – to the despair of rationalists – a largely Christian country. Rudd puts the figure at about 70 per cent, but that's oddly sloppy for a professional politician. The true figure is a still very strong 50 per cent. But the potency of Rudd's appeal to faith is felt even beyond that constituency because, as Marion Maddox explains, even non-believers in Australia admire Christianity:

> Look at atheist parents who send their children to church schools and agnostic voters who support contracting out welfare to the Salvation Army, Anglicare or Mission Australia. They don't go to church, but they want "values." And they want to be reassured their leaders have some.

Early in his time in parliament, Rudd joined the Monday Night Group, a collection of Christians drawn mainly from Coalition ranks. These were deeply conservative and rather strange figures to sit with each week and swap ideas about life, death and eternity: Ross Cameron, Bronwyn Bishop, the ultra-Catholic Brian Harradine and the man he would one day face across the despatch boxes, Tony Abbott. Membership of the group was another item in the caucus indictment of the Member for Griffith back in those days. "One of my Labor Party colleagues said to me, 'Kevin, never pray with the bastards, because if you do it makes it harder to hate 'em. And half of the business of this place is hating them, because we want their jobs.'"

Rudd had been as shy of discussing his faith as his childhood until politics demanded it. But once the campaign to recruit Christians was underway, Rudd spoke and wrote about his faith in revealing detail. It came to define him as a new kind of politician: soft-hearted, hard-headed, courageous, visionary, even pure. Two women in two remarkable interviews dug down to his fundamental beliefs. To Geraldine Doogue he confessed his debt to his mother's CWA Catholicism:

> When you see people in strife, I cannot be indifferent to that because that's the way I've been brought up. And I've given that as an adult a form of political expression called the Australian Labor Party, which is, by the way, as flawed and as failed as I am. But we try.

Would he be in politics but for his faith, she asked. "That's a fantastic hypothetical," he replied. "Probably, I think. None of us are devoid of ego." Faith, he said, helps him battle pride and keep things in proportion even as it offers glimpses of the sublime. He told Julia Baird on the ABC's *Sunday Profile*: "For me it is pretty grounding and also at a deeper, I suppose philosophical, level it's a deep personal wonderment at eternity."

Early 2005 saw Rudd researching religion and voting patterns and conducting a media blitz starring himself as the Opposition's shadow spokesman for Christ. His immediate target was Howard's moralising version of family values:

> Surely a family's ability to put food on the table is a family value; surely a family's ability to afford proper health care for its children is a family value; and surely making sure our children have access to a decent education is equally a family value.

WorkChoices gave Rudd magnificent opportunities to mock the government when Howard and his treasurer, Peter Costello, demanded, on this issue, the churches keep out of the debate: "The message from Howard to the churches is speak out when it suits the government, but shut up when it doesn't."

Rudd's strategy caused disquiet in Labor ranks, particularly on the Left. For decades the party had had to fight clerics in order to pursue social reform. Battles over abortion, birth control, divorce, drug reform, IVF, censorship, homosexuality etc. had been made hard by the churches. The supposedly secular soul of Labor was always under threat. And here was Kevin Rudd inviting the Christians back in. Rudd argued he only wanted them to be given a fair hearing:

> A Christian perspective on contemporary policy debates may not prevail. It must nonetheless be argued. And once heard, it must be weighed, together with other arguments from different philosophical traditions, in a fully contestable secular polity.

And as always he offered a personal assurance: "I am a Jeffersonian separatist."

Australians warmed to his homemade, rather secular faith. An umbilical cord still stretches to Rome, but he worships with his family in the Anglican Church. "Denominationalism means virtually nothing to me." All claims of infallibility – from popes, bishops and preachers – are absurd. No ecclesiastical authority can tell him what to do or what to believe. Christianity has no monopoly on morality. Man's ultimate guide is an informed conscience. As he prepared to vote on stem-cell research in 2002, Rudd turned to his mother for advice. This was not an abstract issue: Marge Rudd had Parkinson's disease.

> My mother was a Catholic from central casting. Her response when I put to her the question of what I should do in this vote was: "In the great traditions of the Church, Kev, that is a question for your conscience, not mine."

Rudd's record on conscience issues is deeply conservative by community standards but falls short of the rigour demanded by Rome and the Pentecostals. He voted in the end for stem-cell research – "as one of that bill's most reluctant supporters" – but couldn't take a further step four years later and vote for the cloning of human embryos. He voted against euthanasia but supported the use of the abortion drug RU486. His position on homosexuality remains messy. He is not troubled personally – many of his best friends etc. – and does not believe Christ backs the harsh sexual teachings of conservative faiths:

> I see very little evidence that this preoccupation with sexual morality is consistent with the spirit and content of the Gospels. For example, there is no evidence of Jesus of Nazareth expressly preaching against homosexuality.

He sends his best wishes each year to Sydney's Gay and Lesbian Mardi Gras – a practice John Howard abjured – and backed legislation to wipe from all Commonwealth laws the last traces of discrimination against gays and lesbians. But there are limits – personal and political – to his sympathies. He has made no move to bring homosexual men and women under the protective umbrella of the *Anti-Discrimination Act* and he opposes anything resembling gay marriage. On Q&A in May 2008, he dodged the question as long as he could, then, to jeers from the audience, admitted the definition recently introduced into the *Marriage Act* – the union of a man and a woman – "is the position of my party and that is the position I hold personally."

Rudd does what he can to keep off such ground, minimising doctrine and maximising values. Christ's teaching on poverty is where his politics and religion merge most comfortably. It's the gospel of Eumundi, Ashgrove and Nambour; a message of hope for those who have, like the Rudds, "run into one of life's brick walls." In one way or another he has been making the same argument for over thirty years:

> What do you do about people who can't look after themselves? People who are poor? People who are oppressed? Do you walk by on the other side of the road, or do you do something about it? Jesus taught us that love requires action.

But nothing radical. Rudd's drift from Rome had not transformed him into one of those campaigning evangelicals who drove the anti-slavery movement and fought for women's suffrage. Rudd sees himself on a transformative mission, but there will be no upheavals along the way. As one of his aides explained: Rudd is not out to abolish poverty so much as see the poor are treated decently.

Sally Warhaft, eccentric and brilliant editor of the Monthly, was looking for someone to profile Rudd, the man nibbling at Beazley's heels. No writer was right for the job. So she turned to Rudd himself: would he write her a substantial piece on faith? Just as Sunrise had given Rudd his speaking voice, constant practice on the nation's opinion pages had taught him how to write. The 6000 words he gave Warhaft a fortnight later were very fine. The appearance of "Faith in Politics" in the first week of October 2006 caused a sensation:

> Above the Great West Door of Westminster Abbey are arrayed ten great statues of the martyrs of the Church. Not Peter, Stephen, James or the familiar names of the saints sacrificed during the great Roman persecution before Constantine's conversion. No: these are martyrs of the twentieth century, when the age of faith was, in the minds of many in the West, already tottering towards its collapse.
>
> One of those honoured above the Great West Door is Dietrich Bonhoeffer, the German theologian, pastor and peace activist. Bonhoeffer is, without doubt, the man I admire most in the history of the twentieth century ...

Rudd presented himself here as a conviction politician of rare courage. His claim to be following in the footsteps of the great was taken seriously. The essay didn't have to be read: the fact of it lifted him out of the ruck. But on reflection, this fascination with Bonhoeffer was odd for a man with Rudd's ambitions. He wryly acknowledges a martyr's example is not much help for a politician. Bonhoeffer was a brave man on the other side. He wasn't dealing with the moral conflicts that inevitably come with government. He told the truth to a vicious regime and paid with his life. What is it about Rudd and martyrs? It's a fascination that goes all the way back to his schooldays. In the essay he called Bonhoeffer "the Thomas More of European Protestantism." Could there be somewhere in him the death wish of a pious schoolboy: some trace of an old hankering to go out in a blaze of moral glory?

Two months after "Faith in Politics" appeared – provoking news reports, opinion pieces, television interviews, panel discussions and outrage from the Opposition – Rudd defeated Beazley for the leadership. The pollsters had already discovered switching to Rudd would dramatically improve Labor's primary vote – mainly by bringing Christians back into the fold. The claw-back had worked, but more for Rudd than the party: the faithful weren't planning to return to Labor but to Rudd Labor. Twelve months later the election confirmed that "Kevin 07" was catnip for believers. "While the blue-collar workers provided the grunt with the national swing, the religious activists provided the leverage and the key seats," John Black of Australian Development Strategies told the *Australian Financial Review*.

> Black says the profile of the Rudd majority "looks a little like a 1970s Gough Whitlam rally held in a Queensland rural church hall – Blacktown meets Nambour – with high-school educated, skilled and unskilled blue-collar workers sitting side by side with the evangelical and activist religions – and making up the numbers are kids, lots of them, from babies up to ten-year-olds."

The morning after his strange victory speech at the Suncorp Stadium, the Rudds worshipped at their parish church of St John the Baptist, Bulimba. Standing afterwards at the gates the prime-minister elect gave his first press conference. Rather woodenly he listed phone calls received from the great – Bush, Brown, Yudhoyono – and ran through the administrative details of the coming days. He promised to govern for all Australians and departed. It was, in its way, as odd as his performance the night before. The *Age*'s Tony Wright wrote:

> Here he was, the winner, and he was offhand, almost disengaged, not a smile to be had. There was a cold purpose about him … As to any detail, any hint of a spark of humour … nothing doing.

"Politics is about power," Rudd had said nine years earlier when he stood for the first time to address parliament. Now he had power. He appeared not exultant but profoundly satisfied. If the pursuit of power had anything to do with repairing the wreckage of his childhood, then at this moment all the bits and pieces of Kevin Rudd were coming together at last. He was just fifty and had power in his hands.

Prime ministers learn on the job. There is no school to prepare them for the task. That he had taught himself so diligently to be a candidate, a contender and leader of the Opposition did not guarantee he could now teach himself to run the country. But Rudd has form: he had at each step of the way exceeded all expectations. And no prime minister had arrived at the Lodge with a CV quite like his, a point he turned into a *Yes, Minister* joke: "I'm probably the first bloke for quite a while who has been at one stage in his life both Humphrey, Bernard and now the minister, and in this case the prime minister, so there is very little I haven't seen before."

But how would he now reconcile his faith and politics? "Anyone who says that it's easy is not telling the truth," he told Geraldine Doogue. On one hand were "questions of conscience" and on the other "the inherent compromise of the political process." Rather grandly for a party politician he concluded: "I think any person in the public political process must first and foremost answer to their conscience."

Doogue pushed him: did he ever feel his faith being sidelined by politics? "The techniques of politics are mind-boggling," Rudd replied. "And there's a danger that you see at the end of that the suffocation of the soul." Doogue was taken aback. "I mean it," he assured her, "because I've seen it." In others? "Judge not lest you be judged. But it can happen. And I think when you sense the extinguishment of the light or the message inside of you in terms of what you want to do for the community – and the country and beyond the country for the world – it's time to pack up and go." But Rudd has a problem: the backers he finally found for himself in the party don't think like that. The NSW Right pursues hard-line, nuts-and-bolts politics. Key figures from the Sussex Street machine are Rudd's advisers. His decent ambitions are at odds with – and appear to have given way to – their "whatever it takes" approach. They don't spend political capital on great moral challenges. What they do best is staying in power. Suffocation of the soul comes with the territory.

Rudd has delivered for Christians. He inhabits that prudish world where respectability, upbringing and faith merge in a kind of resolute caution. This informed his instinctive response to the Henson photographs and to radio foul-mouth Kyle Sandilands quizzing a young girl about rape: "Really off." Decent prudishness is the common spirit of his government and Howard's. So is a meagre commitment to liberty. Christians are not by nature on the side of freedom: they have dedicated their lives, after all, to serving the greatest power known, Almighty God. Rudd's government is bravely facing down all opposition to its plans to filter criminal material from the internet – not just child porn but, say, discussion of euthanasia techniques – while abandoning plans for a timid charter of rights.

On 22 November 2009, Rudd addressed the national conference of the Australian Christian Lobby. His mission: to announce Labor would provide another $42 million to bankroll the National School Chaplaincy Program until the end of 2011. Howard's original scheme was greeted with public protests. This is not the state funding church schools to teach, and church hospitals to treat the sick. The High Court has blessed such arrangements. This program bankrolls chaplains to be chaplains.

Rudd is unperturbed by such naked funding of religion by government. He clings stubbornly to his claim of Jeffersonian purity while acknowledging tacitly that no such scheme would be allowed under the US Constitution. Here in Australia, Rudd argues, the scheme is rescued by choice: schools can choose the denomination and faith of the chaplains. "The Australian attitude to these things is, I think, quite practical," he told me. "The dividing line in this country is not providing anyone a platform to mandatorily impose a religious view using the agency of the state. That principle is alive and well. That is the dividing line." He is equally unperturbed by the constitutional challenge to the scheme now underway. "That's why we have the High Court."

In Opposition no policy was more firmly at the centre of his Christian agenda than the humane treatment of boatpeople. It is the unhealed wound of Australian politics. He wrote in the Bonhoeffer essay:

> The biblical injunction to care for the stranger in our midst is clear. The parable of the Good Samaritan is but one of many which deal with the matter of how we should respond to a vulnerable stranger in our midst.

Even so, Rudd was responsible for the expensive vaudeville of processing on Christmas Island and had talked tough on the eve of the 2007 poll about perhaps towing boats back to Indonesia. He declared people smugglers "scum of the earth" who might "rot in hell" and his government is now considering legislation that would throw Oscar Schindler in the clink. But even now he talks of following the example of the Good Samaritan.

Why not Christ, I asked the prime minister. Wasn't he a refugee? Didn't he only survive to do his work because of the generous refugee policies of Egypt? Rudd wouldn't play: "I'll leave the theological analogy to yourself."

He is hardly more comfortable with the politics. Ask about the passions generated by boatpeople and he replies curtly: "The Australian people will react as they choose fit. All I can do is respond to the objective facts concerning the numbers." He rattles off figures. But there is no fight in the man here, no sign he's willing to mount a bigger political or moral argument to rein in these passions. He presents himself as a spectator at the wreck. "How [the numbers] are reported and how they are responded to by the wider public, that's a separate matter over which I have no control."

But couldn't he use his authority as prime minister to urge Australians to calm down? He dismisses the idea as pointless, indeed counter-productive. He suggests I read Hansard. "I would draw your attention to what I have been saying consistently for a long time, a long degree of time."

Perhaps admitting this country has racial anxieties is the one thing a leader can never do? "If you have a view of the Australian heart and soul, which I think I do – as someone who's grown up in rural Queensland, worked abroad, works nationally – this is a very good-hearted country. There are always going to be people who have real fears and anxieties in any country. You see that throughout Europe; you see it throughout North America; you see it elsewhere in the world as well. But this is a very good-hearted country with a deep instinct for a fair go at home and abroad."

But that, of course, is not what the polls say. Rudd knows it, for a couple of days after our conversation the processing of all Sri Lankan and Hazara boatpeople was suspended indefinitely. The overflow from Christmas Island was flown to John Howard's mothballed detention centres in the desert. In the face of tough polls after a brutal campaign over the boats led by another professed Christian, Tony Abbott, Rudd had caved in. The more humane policies of the new government had lasted barely twenty months. Faith had not sustained him. The old days were back.

Only recently I stumbled on some video of Rudd promising the same Australian Christian Lobby that Labor would, if elected, abolish John Howard's harsh refugee regime. They were pleased. Rudd is thought to be hardly touched by time, but this is footage of a younger man. A few years in government have changed much and aged him. But in August 2007 he answered the lobby's questions with steady confidence:

> I want to make sure this country maintains an open heart ... If we are seen to walk away from all of that, it says something very bad about us internationally. But even worse than that, if we as one of

the initiators of the post-war Refugee Convention consensus are seen to be fragmenting it at the edges, we are also part and parcel of fragmenting the global consensus and machinery for dealing with refugee challenges into the future. I never want to be part of any such government that does that.

Canberra was Brisbane all over again. The same demands, the same chaos, the same kids' brigade, the same high hopes, the same obsession with the news cycle, the same delays, the same business of keeping people waiting – for several hours in May 2008 the chief of the defence force, Air Chief Marshal Angus Houston – the same certainty of being on a great transformative mission, the same ceaseless work – but much, much more power.

Labor had never given such muscle to a prime minister. With victory approaching, Rudd insisted the old tradition of caucus electing the ministry would end. He said: "Part of modernising the Labor Party is putting all that stuff behind us." The power the factions lost, Rudd gained. All but a few heavyweights sitting at the Cabinet table owed their place to him. It has never been harder for Labor ministers to stare down a prime minister.

Nor have Labor Cabinets ever been so circumscribed. From the time Rudd's government faced its first crises, more and more big decisions were made by four key ministers alone – Rudd, Gillard, the treasurer, Wayne Swan, and the finance minister, Lindsay Tanner – sitting as the Strategic Priorities and Budget Committee. In early 2010 Laura Tingle reported:

> When ministers arrive for federal cabinet meetings, they find a folder waiting in their spots which they can look at but not take out of the room. Inside are decisions already taken by cabinet's expenditure review committee and the ultimate power within the Rudd government – the Strategic Priorities and Budget Committee (SPBC). Ministers are expected to endorse the decisions without discussion, and usually do.

Two other Cabinet systems have broken down. Submissions once circulated ten days before Cabinet meetings began to turn up in ministers' offices only the night before. And scrutiny of submissions by inter-departmental committees has largely given way to scrutiny by the prime minister's office and department alone. Rudd is the choke point again.

"This is a Cabinet-led government," he told me. "There are Cabinet meetings each week. There are Cabinet committees who determine the core decisions of the government and that is the way which we have operated this government from the beginning ... I'll be engaged as the chairperson of a number of those committees ... whether it's macroeconomic management, whether it's the investment in and reform of the education system, investment in and reform of the health-care system, whether it's the future of climate change and water – these core decisions of the government, including the national security agenda – surely people would expect that the prime minister was intimately involved in those core agendas as I am through the Cabinet committee structure for which I make absolutely no apology."

Rudd had clearly learnt one lesson from Brisbane, where he earned the nickname "Dr Death" for the ruthless sacking of department heads when Goss came to power. Way down the line, public service bosses were made to re-apply for their jobs. However necessary, this was deeply resented. The slide and fall of Goss can be put down in part to the alienation of Queensland public servants – natural Labor voters and indispensable allies in government. Rudd guaranteed continuity when he came to power in Canberra. While he dressed up the "no spill" principle in the rhetoric of Westminster conventions, the decision to keep Howard's department heads and ambassadors in place was good, cautious politics, however much it distressed the Labor faithful. Bureaucrats under Rudd might find themselves exhausted and baffled by his demands, but their jobs would be secure.

With so much power concentrated in Rudd's hands, access to the prime minister becomes a crucial issue of government. Since before Machiavelli, courtiers have whinged about access. "It's easier to get in to see the Pope than Kevin," one disgruntled backbencher told me. "He's always rushing," a junior minister told me. "You have fleeting meetings." At the top of the ministry is a small group of men and women with easy access to the boss, though it's said there are times and moods when even these heavyweights have trouble getting through the door. They are regarded as conduits to power. John Faulkner told me: "People have come to me and said: will you tell Kevin this? It's presumed I have better access to him. But I say to them: you're the one who should talk to Kevin."

Senior ministers with urgent matters to settle with the prime minister can find themselves waiting and waiting – even flying with their staff to another city only to wait fruitlessly for the door to open. The minister for communications, Stephen Conroy, had to put himself on a couple of VIP flights with Rudd in April 2009 to break the bad news that the tendering process for the national broadband network had failed. "Like most of Rudd's Cabinet ministers, Conroy had trouble finding an opening in the prime minister's program," Peter Hartcher reported in the *Sydney Morning Herald*. Time can also be in short supply for distinguished citizens co-opted by Rudd to pursue his visionary plans for the future. "There comes a point when these big ideas need prime ministerial time, and it isn't there," I am told by Richard Woolcott, Rudd's special envoy to the Asia-Pacific community. "It's a disjunction."

David Epstein, Rudd's chief of staff, bailed out in November 2008. He had lasted a little over eighteen months at Rudd's side, trying to bring order to his office as leader of the Opposition and prime minister. At forty-four, Beazley's former chief of staff was the oldest man close to Rudd. Epstein left before the government celebrated its first birthday. Reports at the time spoke of Rudd still diving into every issue in depth, still not separating wheat from chaff, still operating in logistical confusion. Epstein's place was taken by Alister Jordan. Other staff came and went, but Mr April had lasted eight years to reach the post he had always wanted: chief of staff to the prime minister. He is available fourteen hours a day, seven days a week. He's believed to keep a sleeping bag in the office.

History doesn't worry much about the work practices of the great. Churchill slaved for ridiculous hours and drove his staff to distraction. No one in retrospect gives a damn. Rudd isn't Churchill and this isn't the Second World War, but what looks like dysfunction in Canberra will seem mere eccentricity if the results are worthwhile. Rudd's big brain and

Never again miss an issue. Subscribe and save.

1 year subscription (4 issues) only $49 (incl. GST). Subscriptions outside Australia $79.
All prices include postage and handling.

2 year subscription (8 issues) $95 (incl. GST). Subscriptions outside Australia $155.
All prices include postage and handling.

PAYMENT DETAILS Enclose a cheque/money order made out to Schwartz Publishing Pty Ltd.
Or; Please debit my credit card (MasterCard, Visa or Amex accepted).

CARD NO.

EXPIRY DATE   /   AMOUNT $

CARDHOLDER'S NAME

SIGNATURE

NAME

ADDRESS

EMAIL   PHONE

HOW DID YOU HEAR ABOUT QUARTERLY ESSAY? ☐ MEDIA ☐ WORD OF MOUTH ☐ ONLINE ☐ BOOKSHOP/NEWSAGENT
OTHER:

freecall: 1800 077 514 **fax:** 61 3 9654 2290 **email:** subscribe@blackincbooks.com **www.quarterlyessay.com**

An inspired gift. Subscribe a friend.

1 year subscription (4 issues) only $49 (incl. GST). Subscriptions outside Australia $79.
All prices include postage and handling.

2 year subscription (8 issues) $95 (incl. GST). Subscriptions outside Australia $155.
All prices include postage and handling.

PAYMENT DETAILS Enclose a cheque/money order made out to Schwartz Publishing Pty Ltd.
Or; Please debit my credit card (MasterCard, Visa or Amex accepted).

CARD NO.

EXPIRY DATE   /   AMOUNT $

CARDHOLDER'S NAME   SIGNATURE

ADDRESS

EMAIL   PHONE

RECIPIENT'S NAME

RECIPIENT'S ADDRESS

HOW DID YOU HEAR ABOUT QUARTERLY ESSAY? ☐ MEDIA ☐ WORD OF MOUTH ☐ ONLINE ☐ BOOKSHOP/NEWSAGENT
OTHER:

freecall: 1800 077 514 **fax:** 61 3 9654 2290 **email:** subscribe@blackincbooks.com **www.quarterlyessay.com**

Delivery Address:
Level 5
289 Flinders Lane
MELBOURNE VIC 3000

No stamp required
if posted in Australia

Quarterly Essay
Reply Paid 79448
MELBOURNE   VIC   3000

Delivery Address:
Level 5
289 Flinders Lane
MELBOURNE VIC 3000

No stamp required
if posted in Australia

Quarterly Essay
Reply Paid 79448
MELBOURNE   VIC   3000

prodigious energy save him from many of the perils of his own hyperactivity. When his attention is engaged, he is a formidable distiller of complex information. The process is not efficient and might not end in the best policy, but his understanding of the issues is superb. It all takes time, as an unnamed bureaucrat explained to Laura Tingle:

> You can't go to Kevin and say, "Well, Prime Minister, here is the issue, here are your potential options for dealing with it, here is what we recommend you do, you just sign here," and get it done in a two-hour meeting. He wants to synthesise the information himself, so instead of a two-hour meeting, you'll have a 35-minute meeting where you have to tell him everything known about a subject so that he can go through the intellectual process of considering it himself. Then there will be a few more meetings.

Part of the problem is Rudd's ambition to find "decent" solutions to the nation's problems. Decency is personal, intuitive, hard to delegate. It calls for the sort of scrutiny only he can give. Marry that to a sense of indispensability that is right off the Richter scale, and you have what looks like a recipe for ruin. He takes command of top-shelf policies – the emissions trading scheme or the new health arrangements with the states – but when other policies come under attack, Rudd requires ministers to brief him down to the smallest detail. He responds to pressure by burying himself in detail. This passion to know everything does what it did in Brisbane: makes life around him, and the business of government, hard.

Rudd is proudly the prime minister of fine detail. Mastery of detail ensures good policy outcomes, he told me. It ensures accountability: "The prime minister is required to answer in detail across the entire breadth of government decision-making." So he is satisfied with the flow of business through his office? "Absolutely. There is a structural criticism here which will be levelled at any private office of any head of government, state or federal, Labor or Liberal, which has been around since time immemorial. People should read the literature."

He has never lost his love of showing he knows more than anyone else in the room. Facts pour out of him as they have ever since he was that Jaycees kid speaking for Australia. His Press Club debate on health policy with Tony Abbott in March was a demonstration of how powerfully Rudd can marshal facts. At other times they emerge in a dazzling and somewhat pointless display of mastery. He puzzled James Packer by sitting down with the young gambling mogul one day and telling him everything he knew about gambling in China. His knowledge was encyclopaedic.

Information is a great prerogative of power. Rudd has at his disposal a vast, highly skilled machine for gathering facts. The demands he makes on the public service quickly became legend. So did his chipper response to complaints of bureaucratic exhaustion:

> I understand that there has been some criticism around the edges that some public servants are finding the hours a bit much. Well, I suppose I've simply got news for the public service – there'll be more. This government was elected with a clear-cut mandate. We intend to proceed with that. The work ethic of this government will not decrease, it will increase.

Hours aren't the issue. Bureaucrats don't mind working hard, long days. They object to feeding material in when nothing much comes out; demands made at midnight that might be made at midday; wild flurries of activity driven by petty media squalls; calls for detailed briefing on fourth-rank issues that need never go near a prime minister; and urgent requests for material they know to be sitting in Rudd's office already. They mind *wasting* their time. And they worry that not much good policy can come from a strange mix of rush and delay. The new government was always pressing forward while leaving unfinished business in its wake. Labor had been in office less than a year when Phillip Coorey of the *Sydney Morning Herald* came up with this perfect image:

Rudd is starting to resemble the home handyman in a house full of half-finished jobs, while still eager to begin more. He's out in the backyard building a shed while the wife is yelling at him to finish the kitchen renovation and rehang the screen door out the front.

None of this affected Rudd's popularity for two years. All through this time he was living in a paradise of immense approval. Newspoll had registered something like a national orgasm in his first months in office:

> 84 per cent of us thought him decisive and strong,
> 89 per cent thought him a man of vision,
> 86 per cent though him likeable, and
> 79 per cent thought him trustworthy.

These enthusiasms would cool a little. More of us came to think him arrogant and fewer saw him as a man of vision. But the nation's trust in his intelligence, capability, capacity for hard work and honesty was hardly touched before Copenhagen. Yet Rebecca Huntley of Ipsos Mackay research noticed hesitation in the focus groups. "People warmed to Rudd quickly," she told me. "But the affection hasn't deepened. He's seen as bright, not beholden to the party warlords, competent, his own man, really keen to have the job, a breath of fresh air. But who is he? The feeling is: we've been on lots of dates, but we haven't got to the next level."

First and foremost, he is the engine that drives him. Every witness to his life since Nambour talks about the phenomenal machine inside this man. He turns many faces to the world, but the engine under the hood is the same 5.4-litre V8. What you see of Rudd at any particular moment depends on the destination and the terrain. He is a *sui generis* off-road vehicle whose driver is only glimpsed in passing, a shadow through the windscreen.

He can be so good: turning up without fuss at a bedside or a funeral; sitting on the floor at 2020; delivering the Apology; staying on to yak with the party faithful; charming a table of distinguished Americans at lunch or a bunch of weary doctors in a hospital courtyard; posing time and again for photographs with families and kids when he's out walking; or dazzling a delegation from the China National Peking Opera Company with half an hour's patter in Mandarin.

And he can be so bad. He has a way of ignoring people once their usefulness is past. Before his challenge to Beazley he was ringing John Robertson of Unions NSW half-a-dozen times a day. With victory the calls stopped. He passed in the corridor the man who made him leader of the party without a nod. Text messages to journalists whom this self-confessed media tart had courted for years dried up when he became prime minister. Something of this was inevitable: prime ministers have new and onerous preoccupations. But his neglect of obvious courtesies is a strange flaw in a politician so determined to do his chores perfectly. He switches on and switches off. He shows marked disdain for the feelings of those who are already on-side. It's not clear if their hurt registers. Perhaps other people's feelings are a closed book to him.

He stands on his dignity. He makes a display of little grudges. He is untroubled by the impact of behaviour that is, by any measure, startlingly rude. The party has not forgiven him for failing to turn up to the funeral of John Button, one of Labor's favourite sons, in April 2008. He took a teddy bear instead to the bedside of Cate Blanchett. His request to the BBC not to be seated next to Madam Fu Ying, the Chinese ambassador to Britain – the request was refused – raised diplomatic hackles on a couple of continents in March 2009. The sight of Rudd shuffling his papers as the New South Wales premier, Kristina Keneally, warmly welcomed him earlier this year became a defining bad look of his prime ministership. He and his ministers spent weeks fixing the mess with flowers, smiles and long walks through the grass for television cameras.

He can be beguiling company. His mind is full and rich. He has read a lot and remembered it all. A love of playful argument survives the grinding routine of political confrontation. That he finds being one of the boys so difficult is hardly a hanging offence. Leaders are often awkward in just this way. Those sitting with him as he guzzles peanuts and swears wonder why he tries so hard. It makes people uneasy rather than relaxed. The cussing comes and goes and so does the Australian demotic. Exclaiming "Fair shake of the sauce bottle, mate" on Sky News provoked a torrent of mockery. Defending himself, Rudd let slip a clue to his bifurcated way with words: "I grew up on a farm in country Queensland and my father always used to say, 'Fair shake of a sauce bottle.' I'm the son of a farmer, for God's sake." He never heard such talk from his well-spoken mother, Marge: it's the ghost of Bert Rudd talking to an eleven-year-old.

Everyone wishes he had more sleep. "Kevin starts at around six in the morning," Thérèse Rein told Annabel Crabb. "He might get to bed around one or two, or maybe three. He doesn't need a lot of sleep." That's debatable. From his caucus, his office and his ministry come reports that Rudd is a better man when he has slept. The moods are better, the tantrums fewer, the work easier when he has had something like a normal night's sleep. Moody people are judged – not always fairly – by their worst moods. When Rudd is fresh and things are going well, he turns an open face to the world. Exhausted and under pressure, he shuts down. He is a man who combines resilience and a brittle temper in quite unpredictable ways. On any day he can be both the boyish Tintin of Bill Leak's cartoons and Alan Ramsey's famous "Prissy, precious prick. One with a glass jaw, a quick temper and, when he loses it, a foul tongue."

On a grey afternoon in late January this year, a well-dressed crowd stood on the hard floors of Sydney's Museum of Contemporary Art while Rudd delivered an Australia Day address. He is still as he was at Nambour High: most at home behind a microphone. Delivering speeches seems less a chore for Rudd than one of the perks of office. The Apology will have its place in any anthology of great Australian oratory. Yet Rudd can leave audiences numb with tedium. It is often and rightly pointed out that his syntax owes a lot to *The Book of Common Prayer*, but the strategy of his speeches owes more to the evangelical sermon, which must always, whatever the occasion, spruik for the redeeming virtues of Christ. Evangelists are always on the stump. So is Rudd.

Veterans of the talk circuit swear he spoke for forty-five minutes at the MCA. It may have felt as long but was half that time. This is the authentic Rudd few see and few forget once they have experienced it. He opened with the criminal record of his forebear, Thomas Rudd: five minutes. He mused on the mixture of "can do" and "fair go" that unites Australians: three minutes. A toast at this point would have launched the celebrations nicely, but Rudd was only warming up. An account of the government's triumph over the global financial crisis – four minutes – had guests gazing across the harbour. Surely, surely he would end soon? No. Carefully numbering each step along the way, he addressed the two challenges we face for the future, the three strategic options available and the three measures that must be taken: another twelve minutes.

> In New South Wales, a 123 per cent increase in transport infrastructure; $1.5 billion for the Hunter Expressway; $600 million for the Kempsey Bypass; $1.8 billion upgrading the rail networks in the freight system of this state. Now on top of that when we roll out the National Broadband Network, an investment of up to $43 billion, this state representing a third of the federation will receive the bulk of that investment – altogether with one objective, to increase the state-of-the-art of our infrastructure here and across the country to enable our workers to work more efficiently in the future.

Glasses were long empty. Minds had wandered far away. What on earth did this have to do with Australia Day? The strangeness of such events is disturbing. Surely Rudd knows how boring and out of place this is? How insulting? Has he so little in his mind about Australia that the best he can do to celebrate our national day is give an interim report on infrastructure spending? Is he so vain he thinks he transforms this brass into gold just by delivering it? Or does he not really care what people think? He's there, these are the issues on his mind, and they can listen? He never rescues the situation by being blokey:

> I don't know about you but I'm pining for a drink. I have one further, formal, solemn task to perform and that is to ask you to raise your glasses in a simple toast to our great land, Australia.

Political leaders are born to disappoint. They can never fulfil the hopes they raise. Letting the punters down lightly is a great political art. There are figures in caucus who say: this man has turned out far better than we feared. And there are those who reply: he is as rackety as we feared Latham would be. He is defended by the party, but more out of necessity, it seems, than conviction. He is the leader. Come what may, he must lead the party to the next election.

If disappointment with Rudd has a particular edge, it is because people have come to doubt his courage. Howard's courage was never in question. His values were. The opposite is true for Rudd and doubt is eating away at his goodwill. "What is courage?" Rudd asked at Yarralumla the day Trooper Mark Donaldson was given his Victoria Cross. "The answer perhaps lies best with those who have known the profession of arms." Rudd speaks with ease about the courage of nurses, fire-fighters, police and soldiers, but not often of politicians. He speaks of Australia being shaped by three great values: courage, resilience and compassion. He recognises what courage is: "Knowing the dangers that lie ahead on the road, but defying those dangers and taking the decision to proceed."

He is courageous pursuing those gut issues that connect somehow to the mess of his early years: child protection, education, health, homelessness and China. Signing up to Kyoto and making the Apology were symbolic acts of great distinction, though by the time they happened most opposition had melted away. The polls gave Rudd permission to sign up and say sorry. He shows little ticker for brawls over big abstract issues that go to the soul of the nation. The rights agenda has been casually junked. The republic is postponed to a date to be fixed.

A shrewd old bureaucrat who has worked with a few prime ministers wonders if Rudd really understands the way power works at the top. He isn't afraid to pick a fight but doesn't then behave like a prime minister: he involves himself so much; puts himself on the line so quickly; doesn't exercise authority by keeping his distance. These problems of technique are odd in a man who has had a long fascination with power. Tracking down the powerful, picking the people he has to know, began as a diplomatic duty and became a lifelong passion. He is a determined networker. But perhaps it's his deep respect for power that makes him so careful not to put powerful forces offside. His drive to acquire power is extraordinarily strong – the work of a lifetime – but he shows less enthusiasm to exercise it. His instinct is to hoard rather than spend.

Certainly, at first he overrated the power of business. He prides himself on understanding business – and talks of "deep kissing" big corporations – but those who deal closely with him doubt he grasps its inherent strengths and weaknesses. In his first couple of years in office he took business protests too seriously. He jumped when they barked. His emissions trading scheme was almost whittled away to nothing as a result. Now he has picked a brave fight with the mining companies to tax their mega-profits. A leader with a reputation for cutting and running has set himself a defining test of courage.

"My name is Kevin," he quipped as he greeted the party's national conference in 2007. "I'm from Queensland and I'm here to help." He's not good at jokes. But the limits of Rudd's courage can't be grasped without remembering he comes from up there: he's a son of the DLP, nephew of the Country Party, raised in a state where Labor had been on the outer forever. A Labor grandee told me: "Rudd seems to measure what's worth fighting for by Queensland standards. Never forget the extraordinary caution of Queenslanders." And hovering over Rudd are the failures of the Goss enterprise: all that effort to craft evidence-based policy and the people turned against them. On the tenth anniversary of Labor coming to power in Queensland, Rudd admitted failings – not his but Wayne

Goss's: "His belief in what was good policy would often obscure what many regarded as that which was politically sustainable." So what lessons did he learn about himself from those years? He admits to none. He defends his methods and his policies. The way he sees it, Queensland had a brief interregnum of National Party rule – the result of a protest vote gone wrong – and has been Labor ever since. The people saw the light.

A few days after being sworn in, Rudd found himself on Sydney's Radio 2UE, where Peter FitzSimons asked: "Will you use the power of your office now to continue investigations into AWB and finally get to the bottom of it?" Rudd waffled:

> I said prior to the election and just after that once we form government – that was only on Monday of this week – we'd take advice on that and that's being prepared. But that will take some time to prepare and to deliberate on. I've regarded that as a, and I regard it still, as a matter of gross failure of public administration ...

Rudd has never done a thing about AWB since becoming prime minister. In the United States, oil executives have served time and companies have paid penalties of more than $100 million for giving kickbacks that were a tiny fraction of the massive sums AWB paid to Saddam. In Australia, civil charges have been laid against a few of the company's executives, but the searching investigation of diplomats and ministers Rudd demanded in Opposition has never happened. As this essay goes to press, not a soul has been held to account for their role in the biggest corruption scandal in the nation's history. Rudd is not going to hold an inquiry that stares deep into that pit.

Many failures of courage have followed, but confronted with the global financial crisis of late 2008 he displayed true resolve. His response to that calamity was, in many ways, the making of him as prime minister. He had been puddling round until then. Rudd has been condemning the pretensions of neo-liberal economic theory ever since he entered parliament. They were the subject of a second huge essay he wrote for the

Monthly: "Howard's Brutopia." The collapse of the machinery of capitalism proved his worst fears true. He was propelled by the urgent advice of the treasury secretary, Ken Henry, to pour money into the economy. Rudd has never been afraid to spend money. The strategy was decided independently of Cabinet by the Strategic Priorities and Budget Committee, which served to cement in place its key role in the government. Speed was of the essence. But the failures of the home insulation scheme and the schools building program are part of a wider critique of Rudd's passion for speed and the dramatic announcement of programs to start, if possible, as soon as yesterday.

When Rudd talks of political courage, he talks of Gough Whitlam. He is unabashed in his praise. The prose is purple. Hawke and Keating were never so effusive. Whitlam's is one of the few Australian political lives Rudd appears to have studied deeply. They come in order of interest: Whitlam, Andrew Fisher – Queenslander and acolyte of Keir Hardie – and Bob Menzies. Even after all this time, Gough's "audacious and historic" dash to Beijing still fires Rudd's imagination: "That trip took real political courage." Perhaps Whitlam is another of the martyrs he so admires, offering everything for the cause, crashing through or crashing. At the launch of Jenny Hocking's biography of Whitlam in 2008, Rudd spoke in the grandest terms of him having:

> … a political style and a policy program characterised by unbounded optimism, unbounded passion for the progressive political project and an absolute fearlessness in assaulting the citadels of conservative political power.

This wasn't mere sentimental praise for the alert bundle of old bones who had come to the launch in his wheelchair. Rudd sees himself as a progressive nation-builder in the Whitlam mould. "Today," he declared to the solemn crowd, "we continue that tradition, through a new era of national reform." He is way out of his league here, a thought that should surely have crossed his mind as he stood at the microphone reciting

Whitlam's radical record. Only in one sense is he truly Whitlam's heir: in his dealings with China.

At Peking University in March 2008, Rudd directly admonished the Chinese government for its human-rights record in Tibet. He did so, he said, as a true friend, or *zhengyou*:

> A partner who sees beyond immediate benefit to the broader and firm basis for continuing, profound and sincere friendship … It is the kind of friendship that I know is treasured in China's political tradition.

His courage that day was recognised around the world. In April this year he repeated those words, birched China once again for its human-rights record and deplored the country's friendships with "Regimes around the world that others seek to isolate because of their assault on the integrity of the international system – from the Sudan to Burma." To those who say he has no great plans as a leader, Rudd replies that he is keeping an eye on China. What will our world be like, he asks, when China is once again the great power it was three centuries ago?

The defining failure of Rudd's time in office was the slow collapse and abandonment of his plans to address global warming. Another of the eloquent passages in the Bonhoeffer essay – a document which seems now to have been written in another age – urged Christians to "speak robustly to the state" on climate change:

> The planet cannot speak for itself. Nor can the working peoples of the developing world effectively speak for themselves, although they are likely to be the first victims of the environmental degradation brought about by climate change. Nor can those who come after us, although they are likely to be the greatest victims of this intergenerational injustice. It is the fundamental ethical challenge of our age to protect the planet – in the language of the Bible, to be proper stewards of creation.

Outside Australia he would face formidable obstacles – the intransigence of US industry and of China's leaders – and by the time he left for Copenhagen the political obstacles within Australia were hardly less daunting: the Opposition had risen against his emissions trading scheme, deposed its leader and installed a cadre of climate change deniers intent on blocking the legislation. But even before these political obstacles became perhaps insurmountable, Rudd had shown a particular lack of courage in formulating Australia's response: two years of lobbying by the country's most powerful corporations had left the ETS in tatters. Instead of deterring dirty industries from burning carbon, Rudd's scheme would subsidise coal burning for decades. Trade-exposed industries were to be given free permits galore. So massive were the subsidies proposed for power generators that they drew a public rebuke from the extraordinarily discreet adviser to the government, Ross Garnaut:

> There is no public-policy justification for $3.9 billion in unconditional payments to generators in relation to hypothetical future "loss of asset value." Never in the history of Australian public finance has so much been given without public-policy purpose, by so many, to so few.

The result was a messy, expensive policy the public could neither grasp nor enthusiastically rally behind. This was diplomacy more than politics. Everyone signed. Face was saved. Whether the scheme would work was a second-order issue. It promised to achieve so little at such cost that the failure of Rudd's efforts at the Bella Center in December 2009 was greeted with relief by many who think, as Rudd perhaps still does, that global warming is the greatest economic and moral issue of our time.

When he abandoned the ETS in late April, relegating it to the Siberia of his late second term, scorn poured down on Rudd's head. He was clearing the decks for the elections; he had a brawl on his hands with the mining industry; he had a new national health agreement to bed down and a budget to introduce – but the decision to abandon the ETS was greeted with contempt. He collapsed in the polls. The conviction politician was seen as a man of empty words. His love affair with the Australian people – always more respectful than romantic – has hit a rough patch. For the first time since he became Labor leader, the people are thinking of voting for the other side.

FACE TIME

The manager of this waterfront pub in Mackay has put on a few jewels and stationed herself in the foyer to miss none of the fun. Prime ministers and their staff are not her usual line of work. "We serve the miners," she explains. The place is frantic. Aides come and go, sometimes in running gear but always on their phones. Out on the terrace where things will turn ugly later, Rudd holds court with the usual suspects: the mayor, the editor of the local paper and the Labor candidate. Mackay needs a big new road to get coal trucks to the wharf. The price is high. Alister Jordan takes notes. Waiting patiently to shuttle Rudd's people around the town is a taxi driver who has, at his own expense, packed an esky of ice-cold mineral water for his passengers. He says: "I've been Labor all my life."

At sundown Rudd suggests a walk and we set out in bare feet along the weed-strewn beach. Security guards walk at a distance fore and aft. A passing straggler calls out: "You are the best prime minister ever." The clichés of the day drop away. He talks about himself as a child with great affection but oddly, as if that kid in Eumundi was someone else entirely. The memory of Ashgrove is still blazing away. He was a sick kid then, he says, but he is someone who has grown stronger as he grows older. By this time he is puffing a little as we slog along the sand. That Rudd is still a puritan is beyond doubt, but he's not the prig who preached in Burgmann College. Prime Minister Rudd isn't touting the virtues of Calvin's Geneva. He laughs to hear some think he is a creationist. Not true. Once or twice he shies away from questions, declaring he's just not a reflective person. I don't believe him: I sense no one is more curious about the mysteries of Rudd than Rudd himself.

People come out of the dark to shake his hand. He grabs young kids with obvious delight. Perhaps the happiest version of himself is Rudd the father. Rudd the leader is a loner: it's been a lonely business all along and gets lonelier the higher he climbs. "I think it's just inevitable. Ultimately you have to make calls. And that is an individual and solitary business."

So many of the people I met writing this essay spoke of Rudd as a loner, but not a loner by choice. They see him wanting, if only he knew how, to be part of the in-crowd – in the Nambour playground, in Goss's office and in caucus. A man who has taught himself so much appears not to have been able to master this: the business of belonging among his fellows. It is one point on which even colleagues who despise him feel human sympathy. He seems so stubbornly alone.

There is no force-field around him. As we eat dinner, people drop by the table to chat. "I'm Kevin," he says. They know. Years ago when he was first presenting himself to the public as a human being, he was asked to name his favourite book, film and composer. The list has changed since 2003. *The Brothers Karamazov* now trumps *Crime and Punishment*, *Babette's Feast* beats *Dr Strangelove* – though his eyes light up at the memory and his right hand half-rises in a Nazi salute – and Mozart is now the master, not Beethoven: "Over Easter I listened to the Requiem again and it's just sublime." The painters he most admires are the pre-Raphaelites. "They saw poverty for what it was and had, you know, certain Christian overtones." I struggle to remember something from my childhood: the knock at the door? "Yes, *The Light of the World*." And out pours the history of Holman Hunt's image of Christ standing with a lantern in his hand knocking at an overgrown doorway: one of the great recruiting posters of Christendom.

Almost as he is leaving the table he asks me the argument of this essay. It's a man-to-man question, so I tell him. I'm pursuing the contradictions of his life: the farmer's kid who runs away to China, the politician unloved by his own caucus who turns out to be such a potent electoral asset; a decent man with decent political ambitions who leaves so much wreckage in his wake; an orator of skill who can be a bore; a man with modest policy ambitions but a strong drive for power. And I'm wondering if his government will go the way of Goss's.

I don't notice his face changing at first, but by the time I finish giving this bare-bones account I realise Rudd is furious. I have hurt him and he is angry. What follows is a dressing down which registers about a 3.8

on his Richter scale. He doesn't scream and bang the table as he does behind closed doors. We're in the open. The voice is low. He is perfectly composed. From the distance of the next table it would be hard to tell how furious the prime minister is. Indeed, some boys come over in the middle of it all to ask to have their picture taken with him. Later, he says politely and returns to his work. What he says in these angry twenty minutes informs every corner of this essay. But more revealing than the information is the transformation of the man. In his anger Rudd becomes astonishingly eloquent. This is the most vivid version of himself I've encountered. At last he is speaking from the heart, an angry heart.

Face to face, it's so clear. Rudd is driven by anger. It's the juice in the machine. He is a hard man to read because the anger is hidden by a public face, a diplomat's face. Who is the real Kevin Rudd? He is the man you see when the anger vents. He's a politician with rage at his core, impatient rage.

He finishes, leans over the table, shakes my hand and strides inside, walking straight past the boys waiting so patiently for their photograph. An aide rushes after him. He will not come back out onto the terrace. The boys go in to him. A flash bursts inside and the prime minister disappears.

11 May 2010

SOURCES

My thanks to Josephine Tovey, who helped me research Rudd's life and career.

1	Speech to the Bali conference, 12 December 2007.
3	"Why can't we even mention our own targets": *Guardian*, 23 December 2009, 10.
3	"We prevailed": *Australian*, 21 December 2009, 1.
8	*Griffith Review 21: Hidden Queensland*, 2008, 179, 181.
9	"I was the last" and "Have you made" to Julia Baird, ABC Radio, *Sunday Profile*, 5 March 2006; "When he was" in Robert Macklin, *Kevin Rudd: The Biography*, Viking, Melbourne, 2008, 39; "Is it so hard" in *Sydney Morning Herald*, 27 April 2007, 1; "A town of barely" in address at the launch of *Shell-Shocked: Australia After Armistice*, National Archives of Australia Canberra, 12 November 2008.
9–10	Address to the sesquicentenary celebrations of Queensland, reported *Sunday Mail*, 7 June 2009, 53.
10	"Mum would bellow out the window": Macklin, 66.
10	"old-style Queensland": *Compass*, ABC TV, 8 May 2005.
10	"Every branch in me that beareth not fruit": John 15: 1–13 is identified as her favourite passage in the program for her funeral.
11	"Rudd told *Sixty Minutes*' Ellen Fanning": as quoted by Piers Akerman in the *Daily Telegraph*, 13 March 2007, 20.
11–12	*Women's Weekly*, January 2007, 28.
12–13	All Alan Ramsey quotes: *Sydney Morning Herald*, 31 March 2007, 39.
13	All *Sun-Herald* quotes: 11 March 2007, 10.
13	"a terribly dignifying experience": *Compass*, ABC TV, 8 May 2005.
14	"he told Julia Baird": *Sunday Profile*, ABC Radio, 5 March 2006.
14	*Sydney Morning Herald*, 27 April 2007, 1.
14	"in a dorm with fifty guys": to Cosima Marriner, ibid.
14	"You've always got to be polite": ibid.
14	"It doesn't get much crooker than this": Macklin, 57.
15	"he detested the joint": Marriner, 1.
15	"I watched with wide eyes on the flickering tube": address at the Sir Edward "Weary" Dunlop Asialink Medal presentation to Gough and Margaret Whitlam, University of Melbourne, 6 February 2001.
16	"As a kid growing up in the Queensland country": ibid.
16	"a deep sense of loss of dignity": Baird, 5 March 2006.
17	"in his maiden speech": Hansard, 11 November 1998, 166.

18–19   Chronicle, 25 July 1974, 9.
19–20   "I held it" and "Consternation broke out": from the Asialink address, 6 February 2001.
21   "Through that process": Baird, 5 March 2006.
21   "I was mopping a floor in the emergency department": to me, 8 April 2010.
21   "To escape": quoted in Nicholas Stuart, Kevin Rudd: An Unauthorised Political Biography, Scribe, Melbourne, 2007, 44.
21   Women's Weekly, January 2007, 26.
21   "marvellously snotty": Macklin, 70.
22   "I personally committed to Christ": as quoted by Kate Legge in the Australian, Weekend Australian Magazine, 18 July 2009, 13.
22   "He told me about growing up in Eumundi": ibid.
22   "He dissected the fledgling Fraser government": ibid.
22   Macklin, 115.
23   Jeremy Paxman, The Political Animal: An Anatomy, Michael Joseph, London, 2002, 36.
24   Australian Financial Review, 23 February 2007, 44.
25   "As a possibility, yes": to me, 8 April 2010.
28   "I identified the top forty companies in Queensland": Australian Financial Review, 23 February 2007, 42.
29   "First, to run a traditional Labor government": Sydney Morning Herald & Age, Good Weekend, 1 July 1995, 23.
30   Noel Pearson, Up from the Mission, Black Inc., Melbourne, 2009, 374.
30   "I recall witnessing a 33-year-old Rudd": Pearson, 375.
31   David Malouf, 12 Edmondstone Street, Chatto & Windus, London, 1985, 3.
32   "That was all quietly fixed": Sydney Morning Herald, 15 October 1994, 39.
32   "On the fateful night in 1989": Sydney Morning Herald and Age, Good Weekend, 1 July 1995, 27.
34   "You might like to think about that, Kevin": Australian, 2 September 1995, 8.
34–35   "Queenslanders are sitting on their verandas": Pamela Williams, The Victory, Allen & Unwin, Sydney, 1997, 327.
36   "When my father was accidentally killed": Hansard, 11 November 1998, 163
37   "Politics is about power": ibid., 162.
40   Mark Latham, The Latham Diaries, Melbourne University Press, Melbourne, 2005, 119.
40   "He was a man who": Australian Financial Review, 7 February 2003, 10.
43   Reports of the polls: Australian, 5 November 2002, 1–2; 15 April 2003, 1.
43–44   Age, 18 April 2003, 3.

44	"more votes in the community than in caucus": *Bulletin*, 2 December 2003 (but published a week earlier), 30.
44	*Sunday Telegraph*, 30 November 2003, 4.
44–45	Morgan poll finding 3691, published 30 November 2003.
45–46	Latham, 276.
47	*Sydney Morning Herald*, 25 October 2008, 29.
47	Latham, 365.
48	"Her public support was in the high teens": the polls are Morgan 19–20 January; Newspoll 21–23 January; and Nielsen 21–22 January.
48	"I've got a field marshal's baton": *Courier-Mail*, 25 January 2005, 1.
49	"The terms of reference make it possible": *Australian Financial Review*, 18 January 2006, 4
49	"The prime minister's now routine manipulation": *Monthly*, October 2006, 24, 30.
50	"31 to 27 per cent": *Sydney Morning Herald*, 22 May 2006, 4.
51	"Go for it": *Advertiser*, 17 November 2007, 16.
51	"As a professional of fifteen": *The Howard Years*, Part IV, ABC TV.
51–52	Traits vis-à-vis Beazley and Howard: Newspoll 10–12 November; *Australian*, 12 December 2006, 1. Two party preferred under Rudd or Beazley: Nielsen 30 November to 2 December; *Sydney Morning Herald*, 4 December 2006, 1. Enthusiasm for Rudd–Gillard team: Newspoll, *Australian*, 4 December 2006, 1.
52–53	"Compassion is not a dirty word": Hansard, 5 December 2006, 44.
53	"The man caucus had regarded …": Newspoll 16–18 March 2007; *Australian*, 20 March 2007, 1–2.
53	"A Nielsen poll in June …": *Sydney Morning Herald*, 18 June 2007, 4.
54	"Absolutely revolting": *Daily Telegraph*, 23 May 2008, 4.
56	*Meet the Press*, Channel 10, 7 November 2004.
57	"Rudd was appealing to a bigger audience …": 70 per cent: *Sydney Morning Herald*, 9 November 2006, 17. 50 per cent: Nielsen poll reported in *Sydney Morning Herald*, News Review, 9 December 2009, 1.
57	"Look at atheist parents": *Sydney Morning Herald*, 8 July 2005, 15.
57	"One of my Labor Party colleagues said": *Courier-Mail*, 7 November 2001, 17.
58	"When you see people in strife": *Compass*, ABC TV, 8 May 2005.
58	*Sunday Profile*, ABC TV, 5 March 2006.
58	"Surely a family's ability": *Courier-Mail*, 13 December 2004, 13.
58	"The message from Howard to the churches": *Australian*, 8 August 2005, 8.
59	"A Christian perspective on": *Monthly*, October 2006, 27.
59	"I am a Jeffersonian separatist": *Bulletin*, 2 December 2003, 27.

59	"Denominationalism means": Baird, 5 March 2006.
59	"My mother was a Catholic": Hansard, 6 December 2006, 119.
59	"most reluctant supporters": ibid.
60	"I see very little evidence": *Monthly*, October 2006, 26.
60	*Q&A*, ABC TV, 22 May 2008.
60	"What do you do about people": *Sydney Morning Herald*, Good Weekend, 5 November 2005, 24.
62	"Black says the profile": *Australian Financial Review*, 29 February 2008, 88.
63	"Here he was, the winner": *Age*, 26 November 2007, 2.
63	"I'm probably the first bloke for quite a while": to Laurie Oakes, *Sunday*, Channel 9, 10 February 2008.
63–64	"Anyone who says that it's easy …": *Compass*, ABC TV, 8 May 2005.
65	"The biblical injunction": *Monthly*, October 2006, 29.
65	"scum of the earth …": *Australian*, 18 April 2009, 7.
66–67	<www.acl.org.au/makeitcount/rudd_speech.wmv>
68	"Part of modernising the Labor Party": *7.30 Report*, ABC TV, 29 November 2007.
68	"When ministers arrive": *Australian Financial Review*, 8 March 2010, 1.
70	*Sydney Morning Herald*, 11 April 2009, 9.
71	"You can't go to Kevin": *Australian Financial Review*, 26 September 2008, 52.
72	"I understand that there has been": press conference, 29 May 2008.
73	"Rudd is starting to resemble": *Sydney Morning Herald*, 29 September 2008, 11.
73	"84 per cent of us": *Australian*, 5 March 2008, 6.
73	"before Copenhagen": Essential Report, 7 December 2009.
75	"Fair shake of the sauce bottle, mate": uttered to David Speers, Sky News, 9 June 2009; explained to *Sunrise*, 12 June 2009.
75	"Kevin starts at around six in the morning": *Sydney Morning Herald*, News Review, 18 July 2009, 1.
75	"Prissy, precious prick": *Sydney Morning Herald*, 28 April 2007, 35.
77	"Knowing the dangers that lie ahead": "We Are All in This Together," address at Australia Day citizenship ceremony, Regatta Point, Canberra, 26 January 2009.
79	"His belief in what was good policy": *Australian*, 2 December 1999, 13.
79	Radio 2UE, 7 Dec 2007.
80	"audacious and historic": Gough Whitlam Lecture, University of Sydney, 11 September 2008.
80	"That trip took real political courage": Inaugural Tom Burns Memorial Lecture, Brisbane, 31 July 2008.

80	"... a new era of national reform": NSW Parliament House, 6 November 2008.
81	"Regimes around the world": "Australia and China in the World," 2010 Morrison Lecture, ANU, 23 April 2010.
81	"The planet cannot speak for itself": *Monthly*, October 2006, 28.
82	"There is no public-policy justification": *Age*, 20 December 2008, 21.

WHAT'S RIGHT?

Correspondence

John Hirst

John Howard was the first Australian prime minister to call himself conservative. In Australian political commentary, conservatism is usually seen as laughable or sinister and Howard's espousal of it made denunciation of him easier. It is refreshing, then, to find Waleed Aly and the *Quarterly Essay* taking conservatism seriously and even quoting Howard approvingly. But this is merely a softening-up process; the criticism of Howard soon resumes because, according to Aly, Howard was not a true conservative: he was a neo-conservative. Following other critics, Aly posits a fundamental contradiction between Howard's so-called conservatism and his commitment to a free economy, or neo-liberalism in Aly's classification. An unrestrained capitalism will have a destructive effect on the social order, so conservatives who are also neo-liberals are undermining what they should be protecting and nurturing. Faced with social dissolution of their own making, they respond with strident nationalism and pressures for conformity, and thus show themselves to be not true conservatives but neo-conservatives. This is neat, but it won't survive scrutiny.

Consider these measures of social policy, which Howard implemented:

- Work for the dole
- Tough on drugs
- Against gay marriage
- In favour of fathers having better access to children after divorce
- Intervention in Aboriginal communities in the Northern Territory
- Single mothers to re-enter the workforce sooner
- Better support for families and mothers wanting to stay at home with children

How many of the situations to which these policies were directed were the result of neo-liberal policies in the economy? On my count: none. In different ways they were responding to the libertarian social revolution of the 1960s and 1970s, which was strong in Australia while the economy was still closely regulated. These policies were properly conservative in that they were not trying to restore the status quo but to limit the revolution's effects. So single mothers are not to be stigmatised or denied government help, but they are not to model for their children a life lived on welfare. Homosexuals are not again to be criminals; they can have partners recognised by the state, but they cannot marry. Divorce is to continue on a no-fault basis, but the feminist bias of the Family Court is to be controlled.

Aly makes only one reference to what he calls the sexual revolution, although of course it was a much wider revolution than that. He considers the argument that the recent sexualisation of children might be an effect of the sexual revolution of several decades ago. He rejects this view because the effect is so long delayed; it must therefore be the result of neo-liberalism, which allows business to break any taboo for profit. Of course business has been making money out of the social revolution since it manufactured Che T-shirts and pre-faded jeans. And it is an odd view of a social movement to think its effects must be instantaneous. Social systems have a huge inertia. First a man and a woman might live openly together without being married; after two decades two men may live openly together; after another delay the two men might be able to adopt children; eventually they may be allowed to marry. The libertarian revolution is now meeting resistance but it is not yet a spent force. It is not just business pushing the boundaries with the sexualisation of children; the arts, the entertainment industry and the media are still looking for taboos to break.

I prefer a regulated to an unregulated capitalism, but you can't regulate away capitalism's central dynamic, which is always going to have disruptive social effects. In the long run, as the critics of capitalism long ago predicted, all social relations may be reduced to a cash nexus, but for the moment it is evident that capitalism can operate in a variety of social settings, and it is not wasted effort for economic liberals to have a conservative concern for social health. In times of social disintegration, social democrats should be equally concerned, though some of them have not yet realised it and want to kick on with the social revolution.

Aly makes his contradiction between neo-liberalism and conservatism sharp by assuming that Howard did in fact operate in the economy as a neo-liberal. Though he recognises that ideologies seldom remain pure in politics, he considers WorkChoices as pure a distillation of neo-liberalism as politics is likely to provide. But in actual operation WorkChoices was a massive Commonwealth statute still regulating and limiting the operation of the labour market and providing a variety of entitlements to workers. Aly sees Howard treating workers as little more than units of labour. So whence came the Fair Pay Commission, which continued to set a fairly generous minimum wage? We used to set the minimum wage according to the needs of a man to support a wife and three children in decent comfort. The demands of capitalism have seen that off, but this victory can be offset by supporting through the welfare system those workers on the minimum wage who have family responsibilities – which Howard did in spades.

The Howard policies that most disturb Aly and represent most clearly neo-conservatism and not true conservatism are the putting of pressure on migrants to assimilate and adopt "Australian" values, and the dropping of multiculturalism. Again it is a strain to interpret these moves as a response to the disruptions of neo-liberalism. Aly gives far too little weight to the threat of Islamic separatism. He cites John Stuart Mill against these illiberal insistences on conformity, but how quaint Mill now seems wanting all ideas to flourish so that the truth might be established when we face young men who will blow us up if we don't agree with them or do what they want. The home-grown Muslim bombers in Britain do not overly worry Aly; he considers that there was an "apocalyptic" over-reaction to their exploits. He mentions global terrorism as something that has strengthened the hands of his neo-conservatives, but he will not say "with good reason." Aly is upset that peaceful Muslims in Australia are linked to extremists on the other side of the world. I agree with him that there is less ground for concern about the Muslims in Australia, but he himself makes the point that geography now means little for the formation of identity and cites the emergence of home-grown Islamist terrorism as a prime example. So though Muslims in Australia's suburbs are in a very different social setting from the Middle East or the decaying cities of Britain's industrial north, that gives Australia no guarantee of safety from Islamist terrorism. Aly makes no mention of the conviction in Australia of Muslims for planning terrorist acts. Nor does he address the question to which we all want answers: Is Islam compatible with secular liberal democracy and the rights it protects (including the right to criticise Islam)? Given the tension – to put it no higher – between Muslims and the societies of western Europe, it is quite perverse of Aly to characterise the intensified concern of governments for social cohesion and adherence to the values that sustain a liberal polity as some beat-up to hide the social havoc wrought by neo-liberalism.

Aly is prepared to trust liberalism rather than concocted Australian values, even if embodied in Simpson and his donkey, to hold our diverse society together. He is a great admirer of the civic liberal tradition of the United States and urges us to imitate it. He fails to notice that this tradition is at the core of American nationalism with the heroes, defining moments and soaring rhetoric to make it endlessly appealing and invigorating. Australia has no such national civic tradition; its nationalism has altogether different roots and expression. I could wish otherwise, having worked at the thankless task of civics education in schools.

A new national identity is unlikely to be created by the urgings of a *Quarterly Essay*. Much better to work with what we've got, which is a strong egalitarian tradition which Howard successfully appropriated with his use of "mateship" after the Left stupidly abandoned it because of its past associations with racism and sexism. Egalitarianism can and is being given a stronger civic dimension and is at the heart of Australia's compelling story as the great integrator of migrants.

Aly writes as if there is nothing distinctive about this place; that there is nothing in what we have made of life here that is to be valued or passed on to newcomers. Our past is of no account; there is to be no cultural unity; we are to be merely campers here with the cold comfort of civic virtue. Aly is not true to himself. I saw him on the SBS TV program *Salam Café*, a chat show run by young Muslims, which was knock-about, irreverent and good-humoured in a distinctive Australian way, the successor in this generation to *Wogs Out of Work*. Watching Islam in an Australian idiom made me much more relaxed and comfortable about the future of my country than the formulas Aly advances in his essay.

John Hirst

WHAT'S RIGHT?

Correspondence

George Brandis

Those who brought the Liberal Party into being in 1944 did so with the deliberate intention of creating a liberal progressive political movement which would offer an alternative to the state socialism which they correctly apprehended would define the post-war Labor Party. Liberalism and conservatism had shared much the same political space in the thirty-five years since the Fusion in 1909, under a variety of names and structures – the Commonwealth Liberal Party (Deakin and Cook), the Nationalist Party (Hughes, Bruce and Latham) and the United Australia Party (Lyons, Menzies and once again Hughes) – but none of those precursor parties, beyond a commitment to private enterprise and opposition to socialism, had articulated a clear, well-developed philosophical position.

It was Robert Menzies, after his loss of the prime ministership in 1941, who embarked upon the task not only of reorganising the structure of non-Labor politics, but of giving it an intellectual basis. In the five years between the first of the "Forgotten People" speeches in early 1942 and the first post-war election in September 1946, Menzies, often in collaboration with C.D. Kemp of the Institute of Public Affairs, identified and developed the elements of political liberalism of which the new Liberal Party was to be the custodian and champion.

Waleed Aly describes Menzies' position as "liberal conservatism" and quotes the famous remark, "We took the name Liberal because we were determined to be a progressive party." No doubt Menzies was conservative by disposition and temperament, and liberal conservatism, in the sense Aly uses the term, is a reasonable retrospective characterisation of Menzies' political values. But at the time, the convergence of liberalism and conservatism, which became increasingly evident in the second half of the twentieth century – the "modern marriage," as Aly charmingly describes it – was not as apparent as it is today. Menzies, the senior Victorian in non-Labor politics, saw himself as the legatee of the Deakinite tradition, which certainly owed nothing to conservatism. As Sir Paul Hasluck, the closest thing Menzies had to an intellectual equal in Cabinet, later wrote of him:

> Menzies' political thinking was in accord with the liberalism of Alfred Deakin and the liberalism of late nineteenth-century England ... [A]lthough a traditionalist, Menzies was not a conservative in any doctrinal sense. I do not know what part he had in choosing the name "Liberal" for the new party he formed and led but the name would certainly fit his political creed.

The "Forgotten People" broadcasts – Menzies' most notable testaments of political faith – draw directly upon the English liberal tradition. In the second of the broadcasts (there were thirty-seven in all), he quoted extensively from *On Liberty*, which he described as "full of freshness and truth," and expressly adopted Mill's self-protection principle ("the sole end for which mankind are warranted, individually or collectively, in interfering with the liberty of action of any of their number is self-protection"), describing it as "a pregnant truth ... a good rule, not only of common law but of social morality." By contrast, I have not been able to locate a single occasion when, in a lifetime of speeches and writings, Menzies described his position as "conservatism." Hasluck is incontestably right when he points out that, like Deakin, Menzies drew his political inspiration and values from the liberalism in nineteenth-century England. He was a Gladstonian, not a Disraelian – indeed Menzies' older brother, Frank Gladstone Menzies, was named in honour of the Grand Old Man.

Until the 1980s, all of the subsequent leaders of the Liberal Party essentially accepted the Menzian version of liberalism, which had become canonical. There are two qualifications to that proposition. William McMahon, a more intellectually able man than his parodic prime ministerial image would suggest, was the first significant Liberal to seek to shift the party to a more market-oriented focus. In that respect, McMahon departed from the traditional liberal interventionism which had characterised Menzies' public policy and reflected his Deakinite economic views. In this sense, McMahon anticipated the "dries" by more than a decade, and sounded a distant echo of his fellow New South Welshman George Reid. Secondly, Malcolm Fraser – who, paradoxically, has in recent years come to symbolise small "l" liberalism – was originally, at the time of his clashes with Gorton and his subsequent ascendancy over Snedden and Peacock, seen as a somewhat conservative figure. As prime minister, Fraser was the first Liberal leader to speak of liberalism and conservatism in the one breath. Yet he authored no fundamental departures from the Menzian tradition.

It was John Howard who broke the mould of Menzian liberalism. As the party went through the necessary catharsis of philosophical re-evaluation in the 1980s, Howard changed the Liberal Party's values in two fundamental ways. First, heavily influenced by Thatcher and Reagan as well as by the economic views of Milton Friedman, and eager to distance himself from the quietism on economic reform which had characterised the Fraser government, he adopted the radically pro-free-market agenda of the "dries." This marks the point at which, in Waleed Aly's terms, the Liberal Party shifted from "liberal conservatism" to "neo-liberalism." The principal beachhead was industrial relations reform, then being championed by the H.R. Nicholls Society, with which Howard associated himself. Ironically, it was at the 1986 Deakin Lecture, ten months after he became leader, that Howard delivered the *quietus* to Deakinite liberalism.

The second fundamental change that Howard wrought was to claim conservatism for the Liberal Party as a philosophical co-parent with liberalism.

Howard was the author and advocate of the "broad church" theory of the Liberal Party. Aly appears to equate Howard's conservatism with neo-conservatism. I agree with Aly that, in its sometimes histrionic and belligerent expressions, neo-conservatism is fundamentally discordant with the conservative tradition at its best and most civilised. Although there are some aspects of Howard's policies and rhetoric that fit within Aly's description of neo-conservatism, in my view it is too narrow a characterisation of his social views. Howard constantly invoked the Burkean tradition, and I believe he did so with sincerity. As I argued in my 2008 essay "John Howard and the Australian Liberal Tradition," the governing idea of Howard's social conservatism was his belief in the importance of social cohesion in a society based upon shared values. As he said in his 2006 Australia Day address:

> In the twenty-first century, maintaining our social cohesion will remain the highest test of the Australian achievement. It demands the best Australian ideals of tolerance and decency, as well as the best Australian traditions of realism and balance.
>
> Australia's ethnic diversity is one of the enduring strengths of our nation. Yet our celebration of diversity must not be at the expense of the common values that bind us together as one people – respect for freedom and dignity of the individual, a commitment to the rule of law, the equality of men and women and a spirit of

egalitarianism that embraces tolerance, fair play and compassion for those in need. Nor should it be at the expense of ongoing pride in what are commonly regarded as the values, traditions and accomplishments of the old Australia. A sense of shared values is our social cement.

There is nothing culturally belligerent about sentiments such as those. Social cohesion is an essentially Burkean concept, as is another dimension of Howard's social philosophy: the idea of society as a coalition or partnership. The clearest expression of that view is in Howard's first "headland" speech in 1995:

> One of the defining characteristics of our modern conservative approach is the use of the leadership role of government to actively forge a new social coalition to address modern social problems in a modern way. We believe that Australia's capacity for compassion is not measured by the size of government. Our approach does not entail any winding back of support for individuals and families in need, but it does call for a broader community partnership. Our purpose is to build a new social coalition of government, business, charitable and welfare organisations and community groups … This approach rejects an older view that governments could fix all society's ills if only they allocated more resources … It upholds the responsibilities of government, but acknowledges their limits. It promotes the view that a community most effectively addresses its social problems when all groups, working with government, co-ordinate their strategies and complement their particular strengths.

The social coalition model was seen in a number of the Howard government's policies, for instance the delivery of welfare services through private-sector agencies and the charitable sector. It combines Burkean social theory with liberalism's traditional belief in limited government.

Just as the view of society as a coalition of mutually interdependent elements was traditionally conservative, so was another of Howard's fundamental values: the idea of a mutual obligation between the individual and the community:

> I came to office with a very strong personal commitment to the principle of mutual obligation. Society, in my view, has a responsibility to look after those who are deserving of help. They, in turn,

> have a responsibility to meet reasonable ... requests from society to contribute in return for the assistance they have received.

From this belief grew work for the dole and similar social programs. Once again, there is nothing inconsistent with orthodox conservatism in these beliefs.

It was in some aspects of his cultural politics that Howard came closest to embracing the neo-conservative agenda. Although I think it absurd to claim, as Waleed Aly does, that Howard's view of Australia was as a "monoculture" – it was, after all, on Howard's watch that the number of non-European migrants exceeded those of European immigrants for the first time – I do share Aly's concern that the frequent invocation of "the mainstream" can run the risk of marginalising minorities and playing the dangerous game of suggesting that some citizens are more truly Australian than others. As I wrote in 2008:

> [The] danger is that when the mainstream is identified with the nation, the implication may be that those who are not part of the mainstreams are not in the fullest sense members of the nation ... In an ethnically diverse and culturally pluralistic nation, the danger of the rhetoric of the mainstream is that it involves assuming that some are in the mainstream and others are not, and presupposing which is which. For instance, when Pauline Hanson attacked Asian Australians in 1996, Howard's disappointingly leaden-footed response appeared to suggest, although not sympathy with her point of view, the assumption that her views were legitimate because widely shared. Was Pauline Hanson part of the Australian mainstream? Were those she attacked not?

It is at this point that the Howard era drew closest to the unattractive face of neo-conservatism, which, as Aly rightly argues, is inconsistent with conservatism in its admirable Burkean form.

It is also in their different attitudes to the relationship between minorities and "the mainstream" that neo-conservatism comes most sharply into conflict with liberalism in the classical sense embraced by Menzies. The most fundamental public value of liberalism is the paramountcy of the right of individuals to live their own lives in their own way, without being either preached at and interfered with by the politically correct Left, or bullied into conformity by the belligerent Right. As I argued in my 2009 Alfred Deakin Lecture, the points of tension between liberalism and conservatism occur when the rights of individuals or minorities come into conflict with existing laws and prevailing social customs. When this happens – as it did, on occasions, during the Howard government – merely weighing the rights of the individual in a balance against the mainstream attitudes of society is not an adequate response for a liberal.

As John Stuart Mill wrote in *On Liberty* 150 years ago, in words which could just as well describe the Rudd government:

> [T]here is ... in the world at large an increasing inclination to stretch unduly the powers of society over the individual, both by the force of opinion and even by that of legislation; and as the tendency of all the changes taking place in the world is to strengthen society and diminish the power of the individual, this encroachment is not one of the evils which tend spontaneously to disappear, but, on the contrary, to grow more and more formidable. The disposition of mankind, whether as rulers or fellow citizens, to impose their own opinions and inclinations as a rule of conduct on others, is so energetically supported by some of the best and by some of the worst feelings incident to human nature that it is hardly ever kept under restraint by anything but want of power; and as the power is not declining, but growing, unless a strong barrier of moral conviction can be raised against the mischief, we must expect, in the present circumstances of the world, to see it increase.

The future for the Liberal Party lies in continuing to provide that "strong barrier of moral conviction." To the extent to which Waleed Aly is saying much the same thing, I agree with him.

George Brandis

WHAT'S RIGHT?

Correspondence

Tom Switzer

Even before Barack Obama's presidential election victory and the liberal Democrat stranglehold on the US Congress in 2008, there was widespread talk of the exhaustion of conservatism. Indeed, every new day seems to bring another article or book on the subject – and not just in the United States, but in the United Kingdom and Australia too. And yet, the British Conservatives, if Waleed Aly is to be believed, "will almost certainly remove Labour from government in this year's election." Washington's seasoned observers predict big Republican gains in the US House of Representatives and Senate in November. And polls here show the Coalition, under Tony Abbott, will do much better at the ballot box this year than anyone had the right to expect only six months ago.

Aly's *What's Right?* is the latest publication that peddles a pessimistic outlook for right-of-centre political parties, most notably Australia's Liberal Party. I disagree with his thesis that conservatism has entered a period of turmoil and that right-of-centre political figures no longer have a compelling vision for the future. Still, Aly deserves praise for understanding the origins of political conservatism as well as its relationship with liberalism better than most local commentators in recent times. By putting the philosophy of Burke and Disraeli in its proper historical and ideological context, Aly presents a sophisticated intellectual explanation for what passes as the right wing of the political spectrum in the Anglosphere.

Simply put, true conservatives prefer flexibility and adaptability to rigid consistency and purity of dogma. As the late Harvard political scientist Samuel Huntington identified more than fifty years ago, the antithesis of conservatism is not simply liberalism or even socialism. It is radicalism, which is best defined in terms of attitude towards change. For conservatives, temperament should always trump ideology; and the single best test of temperament is a person's attitude towards change. Aly is right to say that although conservatism accepts the need for change depending on what the circumstances permit and what the priorities of the day demand, it is hostile to disruptive and radical change. After all, it can lead to loss as well as gain, and it is fraught with the danger of unintended consequences. This is why, as Aly kindly reminds readers, I opposed the Iraq invasion in 2003, an unnecessary war against a threat that could have been contained.

Moreover, as Aly points out, political terms are often meaningless and can foster simplistic divisions and create artificial alliances. Indeed, it is not even clear what it means to be on the "Right" on any given matter: Should an Australian conservative take advice from former treasurer Peter Costello or Liberal leader Tony Abbott on paid maternity leave? Should he listen to columnist Andrew Bolt or intellectual Owen Harries on regime change in the Middle East? Should a British conservative heed former chancellor Kenneth Clarke's call to expand integration into the European Union or to Britain's favourite Eurosceptic and rising Tory star Daniel Hannan? Should an American conservative pay attention to Republican congressman Ron Paul on free trade or former Arkansas governor Mike Huckabee's warnings about unfair Chinese trade practices?

Aly's thesis, however, is far from convincing with respect to the policy debates, most notably over the economy and climate change. He appears to subscribe to Kevin Rudd's thesis that the global financial crisis is simply the fault of "neo-liberalism." If anything, as even the formerly strident critic of economic rationalism John Carroll recently conceded, the GFC's roots had more to do with muddled government interference than unfettered markets. In the US, it was a government agency that kept monetary policy unnaturally loose. And it was a Democratic president (Bill Clinton) and a wayward Congress that leaned on government subsidiaries Freddie Mac and Fannie Mae to offer mortgages to people who would never repay them.

Australia, meanwhile, is weathering the financial storm and remains the envy of the industrialised world. This has little to do with Labor's big spending, debt-ridden fiscal "stimulus," something to do with China's thirst for our resources, and nearly everything to do with the starting point. When Australia entered the crisis in September 2008, we had no debt, a decent surplus, a record low unemployment rate of 4 per cent and no banking crises. This impressive record had a lot to do with the free-market reforms of Coalition and Labor governments from 1983 to 2007.

To be sure, these policies – the dollar float, tariff cuts, financial deregulation, tax reform and labour-market liberalisation – amounted to radical change, which created losers as well as winners. (Hansonism, in many respects, represented a backlash against these changes and, in Joseph Schumpeter's language, the "creative destruction" involved in that process.) But by any objective criteria, those historic changes were not only desirable in the circumstances; they also led to the longest economic expansion in our nation's history. From the Keynesian mindset that delivered economic turmoil in the 1970s, Australia had moved to an era of sounder policy and more durable prosperity. Free markets and prudential financial regulatory oversight occupied the moral and policy high ground. Most conservatives supported that agenda, even when the Coalition was in opposition. Far from being discredited, they have been intellectually and politically vindicated.

But it is Aly's assessment of man-made global warming that is particularly odd. He says that "climate change promises to be a more ongoing political conundrum [than the GFC] that will be of lasting philosophical consequence" and could "wedge" the conservative parties in the future. But however much this argument had merit in 2007–09, it increasingly lacks validity in a post-Copenhagen world that does not conform to the expectations of Tim Flannery and Clive Hamilton. Politics, after all, is never fixed; it is always in a state of flux. The only certainty is that the political climate always changes. And the wind, far from blowing conservative parties off the electoral map, threatened to turn into a perfect storm for Kevin Rudd. Which is why he has jettisoned the emissions trading scheme.

During the eighteen months following the release of the Garnaut Report in the winter of 2008, the climate debate in Australia had been conducted in a heretic-hunting, anti-intellectual atmosphere. Rudd had claimed that climate change is the "greatest moral, economic and social challenge of our time" and he even linked "world government conspiracy theorists" and "climate-change deniers" to "vested interests." Much of the media, business and scientific establishment deemed it blasphemy that anyone dare question Labor's grand ambitions.

The Liberals, first under Brendan Nelson and then under Malcolm Turnbull, dithered, equivocated and vacillated over the appropriate response. When the Coalition finally established a policy to back the government's scheme, the party faithful revolted and its base crumbled. Throughout the process, the Opposition was badly trailing Labor in the polls and heading towards electoral oblivion. With Tony Abbott's rise in December, however, everything has changed. The new Liberal leader has not only subjected Labor's agenda to impose potentially crushing costs on business and consumers to some much-needed scrutiny, he has also spelt out in the most forceful and coherent language how the ETS has all the hallmarks of a giant revenue grab and creeping socialism.

Late last year, commentators predicted that the Liberal Party's "ill-judged" opposition to the ETS (Michelle Grattan) would amount to "electoral oblivion" (Peter Hartcher), "humiliation at the polls" (Laurie Oakes) and a "political suicide mission" and "the road to ruin" (Paul Kelly). Today, without missing a beat, the same commentators concede that Liberal opposition to the ETS has "undermined" Rudd (Grattan), "vindicate[d] the politics of the Coalition's decision" (Hartcher) and forced a "running scared" Rudd (Oakes) into "one of the most spectacular back-downs by a prime minister in decades" (Kelly). Polling data confirms this trend: according to a Lowy Institute survey late last year, less than half of Australians consider global warming a serious and pressing problem, and climate change ranked seventh in a list of ten "most important" policy priorities, down from first only two years ago.

Meanwhile, climate-change fatigue is setting in all over the globe. The governments of China and India insist they won't join the West in what they see as an economic suicide pact. In France, the Sarkozy government recently shelved plans to introduce a carbon tax. In Germany, polls show only 42 per cent of Germans worry about global warming. In the European Union, the ETS has been a victim of fraudulent traders and done little to curb emissions. In Canada, climate law is stalled in legislative limbo. Even New Zealanders are doubting the merits of a go-it-alone strategy! In Obama's America, furthermore, the recession, record snowstorms, massive Tea Party rallies, rising public scepticism of climate-change science, mounting industry opposition, climate-gate and glacier-gate scandals – all these have dampened the political climate for a cap-and-trade law. In Copenhagen, the United Nations' climate-change summit went up in smoke. And in Mexico City later this year hopes for any verifiable, enforceable and legally binding agreement to reduce greenhouse gases – and to include developing nations such as China and India that are chugging along the smoky path to prosperity – are a chimera.

In this changing climate, it is not clear how conservatives would win swing votes by championing unilateral action on slashing carbon emissions that would cause economic pain for no environmental gain. In contrast, by no longer being carbon copies of Labor and by forcing the prime minister into a humiliating policy retreat, the Liberals stand a good chance to win back key segments of the lower-middle class and working class – the Howard Battlers – to whom Kevin Rudd appealed in 2007. The point here is that radical change – that is, the ETS – does not sit well with either a conservative party or the conservative tendencies of Middle Australia.

And then, what if the Cassandras are either wrong or have seriously exaggerated the threat? I do not question that the Earth warmed during the last twenty-five years of the last century, but the evidence this century indicates at least a flat-lining of the average surface temperature. Why this is the case is not clear. But even if a scientific consensus exists, a policy consensus most certainly does not. In this environment, a sensible conservative response could involve adaptation – a policy alternative Aly does not even consider – rather than economically crippling and possibly futile grand gestures.

Besides, uncertainties in climate forecasting remain huge. In the 1970s, prominent environmentalists were issuing dire warnings about overpopulation, mass starvation and global cooling. Yet population growth estimates have declined. Biotechnology advances have found ways to feed more poor people than the alarmists predicted. And global cooling has become global warming. Remember the costly and fraudulent scares we have recently lived through, from mad cow disease to genetically modified foods. As the English prime minister Lord Melbourne once said: "What all the wise men promised has not happened, and what all the damned fools said would happen has come to pass." Bear all this in mind when you hear Waleed Aly dismiss conservatives as "deniers" and justify interventionist policies in the name of solving a speculative problem that would lead to radical and disruptive changes which, in turn, could have a substantial and detrimental impact on the lives of the Australian people.

Tom Switzer

WHAT'S RIGHT?

Correspondence

Andrew Norton

Early in his essay on the future of Australian conservatism, Waleed Aly remarks that it wasn't clear what right-wing critics of Kevin Rudd's *Monthly* essay on "neo-liberalism" thought the term actually meant. A few of us had been watching the word "neo-liberal" spread through left-wing analysis of the free-market movement, but Aly has a point to which he should have paid more attention. If most candidates for being Australian neo-liberals aren't sure what neo-liberalism is, can it be a useful concept for analysing Australian politics?

I think the answer to that question is no. As Aly and many others use "neo-liberalism," it is associated with beliefs that few or no people hold. Who believes, as Aly suggests that neo-liberalism maintains, that nothing is valuable unless the market assigns it a value? He cites no sources on this, and even within the individualist framework Aly attributes to neo-liberalism it cannot be correct. Markets assign exchange values, the prices on which buyers and sellers can agree. But prior to this must be the values set by individuals. Culture, sentiment and ethics can all give things a value above money, blocking any exchange. There is a big difference between permitting exchange of goods or services for money, and believing that the market price reflects their only value.

Aly claims that "neo-liberalism easily collapses into a theory of pure individualism that risks doing away with society altogether." Here Aly quotes Margaret Thatcher's famous "there is no such thing as society" interview. The point Thatcher was trying to make – admittedly not clearly expressed – was that there is no abstract "society" responsible for taking care of every problem. Real people pay for any entitlements coming from the state. She talks about families, neighbours, charities, and responsibilities to others, part of what "society" means in ordinary language. It is a long way from Aly's later claim that neo-liberal politics has almost nothing to do with consideration for others.

For Aly's essay, the bigger problem is that this line of criticism doesn't fit with his later analysis of Australian politics. When he turns to the Howard years, his complaint isn't that the Howard government lacked a concept of society, but that it had too much of one. He accuses it of wanting to foster "monoculturalism," and engaging in an "extensive and often belligerent 'Australian values' campaign." If the Howard government didn't engage in a neo-liberal attempt to do away with society, and Aly cannot nominate any Australian intellectual as believing such a thing would be desirable, does this idea belong in an essay on Australian politics?

Aly says neo-liberals believe that markets cannot have negative consequences, leading them to deny climate change rather than admit corrective action is required. But again we have dubious intellectual history and a lack of Australian evidence. If the idea of "negative externalities" – as economists call costs like environmental damage – isn't part of neo-liberal thinking, we have to exclude the vast majority of economists from neo-liberalism, since this idea is a standard one in the neo-classical economics taught at most Australian universities. The late Milton Friedman, perhaps the single most important figure in the revival of free-market thinking, argued half a century ago that there are environmental consequences from market activity that governments may need to remedy. The example he gave was pollution in a stream. If Friedman can't be called a "neo-liberal," who can? While some generally pro-market intellectuals and politicians in Australia are climate-change sceptics, Aly offers no evidence that this is because they believe, in principle, that no market corrections are ever required.

While Aly's neo-liberal framework again doesn't explain what is going on in Australian right-of-centre politics, he is undoubtedly right that climate change has "driven a wedge through conservative politics." It is rare for Liberal leaders to lose office on a specific policy rather than on general performance, but Malcolm Turnbull's support for an ETS last year cost him his job in a close vote. This division is consistent with the results of an online survey I conducted in early 2009. Among the people identifying as classical liberal or libertarian (tellingly, nobody called themselves a "neo-liberal"), 9 per cent thought climate change wasn't happening, 32 per cent thought it was happening due to natural causes, and 42 per cent thought it was happening due to human causes. Policy responses were even more divided. Of those choosing one of the alternatives offered in this question, a small majority favoured action but were split between a carbon tax (33 per cent) and an ETS (24 per cent). Those against action were split between opposing it because the costs of action exceeded the benefits (27 per cent) and because there was not a problem to be fixed (17 per cent).

Aly thinks that a conservatism freed of neo-liberal influences would help conservatives deal with the climate-change issue. He may be right that conservatives would have less internal difficulty with climate-change politics without the influence of free-market supporters, but not in the policy direction he anticipates. Of the people who chose conservative labels in my survey, 20 per cent thought that climate change wasn't happening and 51 per cent thought it was happening but due to natural causes. Pro-climate-action arguments come mainly from people on the free-market side, and conservatives would be more united – though probably not closer to the best policy response – if they flew solo on climate change.

The idea of "neo-liberalism" gets in the way of good analysis of Australia's last quarter-century. While markets have replaced bureaucratic control in some areas of the economy since the early 1980s, the often outlandish beliefs Aly and others associate with neo-liberalism cannot explain this fact. I believe analysing the push for free-market policy change needs to start by seeing it as an issue movement rather than as a single ideology. As with other issue movements, such as environmentalism or feminism, the unifying feature is a broad cause and policy direction, and not a common orthodoxy. The intellectual revival of classical liberal and libertarian ideas and intellectually confident neo-classical economists helped put market ideas on the policy agenda. But the actual implementation was largely carried out by self-described social democrats and conservatives, with each group having its own pragmatic rather than ideological reasons for needing to reform particular industries or improve Australia's economic performance. Good history requires looking at why people acted the way they did from their own perspective.

Waleed Aly, and the many other academics offering similar accounts of Australian politics, should throw out any material relying on "neo-liberalism" and start again with the actual words of the many Australians who, over the last forty years, have called for free-market reforms.

Andrew Norton

WHAT'S RIGHT?

Correspondence

George Megalogenis

I don't have a criticism of Waleed Aly's essay, and must declare upfront that he is a friend and fellow Richmond tragic. But a heretical thought popped into my head when he argued that "things changed around 2007."

Intuitively, Aly is spot-on: we are in a new era. He writes: "The issues that had dominated politics in the English-speaking world – terrorism, the war in Iraq, the culture wars – began to lose their urgency and political purchase." Aly offers three examples of the post-terror phase of English-speaking politics. They are Barack Obama's rise to the US presidency in 2008 – "a candidate with no compelling foreign policy credentials [who] defeated a former war hero, John McCain" – Gordon Brown's rebuff from conservative politicians and a cynical media when he tried to toughen Britain's anti-terror laws, and Kevin Rudd's eclipse of Howard in 2007.

All true. But as I read this passage, I remembered that George W. Bush had done something similar to Obama. Bush neutered McCain in the primaries for the Republican presidential nomination in 2000. He then took his giant-killing form to the general election, where he prevailed against Democrat opponents with much longer CVs – Al Gore in 2000, and John Kerry, another war hero, in 2004. Bush relied on fractions of the American population to form his majorities, most notably conservative church-goers.

Obama campaigned on single-word slogans: "Hope" and "Change." He energised the disengaged and disenfranchised. He was, like Bush, a god-like hero to his supporters, and a villain to the other side. His majority was, like Bush's, an alliance of minorities. Only Obama's base was racial, not religious – blacks, Hispanics and Asians.

Politics has always flirted with the worst aspects of marketing, but the Left suffers a form of selective amnesia whenever it beats the Right at its own game. "Kevin 07" was excused because Labor's slogan was a cheeky means to a worthy end, the removal of a long-term government. But when the snake oil was in the other hand, for instance Howard's "For All of Us" in 1996, the Left complained that he was dog-whistling. Howard's battlers were belittled as swing voters because they were motivated by revenge. Rudd's youth belt was written up as an agent of generational change.

Okay, so I've surrendered to these clichés from time to time. My point is that winning elections requires equal measures of bullshit, bastardry and good luck. Ideology doesn't come into it. But we are compelled to assign a higher meaning to the results because a nation reveals a little more about itself each time it votes.

Australia swung sharply right in 1996, then turned again in 2007. That's the easy part of the analysis. Yet the successful Opposition leader in each case signed up for 90 per cent or more of the incumbent's agenda. Howard drove Paul Keating mad by agreeing with him, from Medicare to *Mabo*. Rudd was sold as a younger version of Howard. The real changes came in government, not in the campaigns themselves. But we have no simpler device for dividing the eras than by elections.

Australia's political cycle is rarely in sync with that of the United States or Great Britain. When Ronald Reagan and Margaret Thatcher became free-market revolutionaries in the 1980s, Australia joined the club from the Left. It was Bob Hawke and Paul Keating who did our deregulating.

More recently, Bush had Howard, and together they went to Iraq. But their economic policies were poles apart. Bush crashed the federal budget; Howard left behind a surplus. Where Howard did try to mimic the US, on workplace relations, the electorate pulled rank and sacked him. Australia has always been a little more left than the US, which is why the coincidence of Rudd and Obama is so fascinating.

But as Aly reminds us, the concepts of Left and Right are next to meaningless.

Bush is easily reduced to policy buffoon because his presidency was bookended by two bubbles: the tech wreck of 2000–01 and the global financial crisis of 2008. The first wasn't his fault. But the second has his name on it. The GFC is, of course, neo-liberalism's nadir – until you remember that Bush's most direct contribution to the sub-prime lending crisis was a socialist objective to increase the home-ownership rates of "minorities" – that is, blacks and Hispanics. The housing boom spared Bush in 2004, as it did Howard.

Against Bush, Obama is easily elevated to the status of political intellectual. But are these two presidents really so different? Both men are career politicians, more comfortable campaigning than governing. Obama's lack of experience didn't matter at the ballot box because he was selling something unusual, the notion that he was too smart to be just another politician. The dummy Bush made the genius Obama, just as the amoral Bill Clinton made family man Bush eight years earlier. None of these pitches had anything to do with policy.

Now the paradox: the optimist in me looks forward to a more ideological era. The phase that ended with the GFC was maddeningly inconsistent. The electorates here and in the US weren't interested in ideas, they just wanted to see the money. The lines between Left and Right blurred precisely because the public wanted it every which way. Both sides deferred to the hip pocket, and where that didn't work, to jingoism. This was a classic case of tail wagging dog.

The explosion in public debt that has followed the GFC will force all democracies to reconsider the role of government. This has the potential to put belief back into the two-party system because neither side can afford to be all things to all voters in quite the same way again.

George Megalogenis

WHAT'S RIGHT? | Correspondence

Jean Curthoys

On first impression, Waleed Aly's essay looks like an Australian version of the "red Toryism" supposedly re-invigorating conservative politics in Britain. This is not because it rejects neo-conservatism and neo-liberalism in the name of a genuine conservatism, for that is now an established genre – there are, at least, the American "paleo-conservatives," British thinkers John Gray and Roger Scruton, not to mention Australia's Owen Harries. It is because Waleed Aly's conservatism, too, has a distinctly "pinkish" aspect. Like the red Tories, he would reduce economic inequality, is comparatively friendly to trade unions and is seriously concerned about the environment. And like them, he does not seem at all inclined to potentially blood-and-soil notions such as "rootedness" (the paleo-conservatives) or "love of land" (Scruton) to found his conception of society and citizenship.

First impressions are misleading and this one profoundly so. The pivotal question for conservatives concerns how citizens are, or ought to be, bound together into a social whole and Waleed Aly's answer is diametrically opposed to that of the red Tories. His advocacy of a "civil identity" is based in a passionate liberalism, the central concern being with the limits of government, not in the neo-liberal sense of small government, but in the classical liberal sense that the ideas, values and attitudes of citizens are not its business. His argument implies a distinction between society and communities, the former the legitimate concern of government, the latter not. For the crucial feature of his "civil identity" is that it relates only to society, constituting the identity of citizens *qua* citizens, and leaves untouched other cultural or religious values a citizen might have and around which, he thinks, communities form organically. By contrast, David Cameron's advocacy of a "big society," which is informed by the red Tory notion of a "civic state," is one in which government takes upon itself the responsibility of renewing communities, employing for that purpose an "army of professional community workers" with the aim of having every adult citizen active in a community group. Here, community and society elide into a communitarian nightmare.

The most powerful part of Waleed Aly's polemic is his condemnation of the Howard government's "Australian values" campaign, not on the grounds that it was silly, though it was, but because it flouted two fundamental liberal principles, namely freedom of thought and the protection of minorities. It is a significant argument because it reveals that, contrary to the received wisdom that liberal principles are jeopardised by the presence of cultural minorities, these minorities have a real interest in upholding just these principles. When the state moves beyond enforcing the law to imposing the "right" attitudes, be they "Australian values" or more "politically correct" ones, it is these minorities in particular which stand to be either humiliated or patronised, if not demonised. The contrast between this "intelligent voice of Islam" and the new Tories emerging from Britain's cultural mainstream is instructive. For the latter have forgotten their liberal heritage and are all too keen to have government lecture citizens on their attitudes, on their personal morality, their belief in God, and their involvement in local communities.

Where, then, is the conservatism in Waleed Aly's "future of conservatism"? It is manifest in the recognition (among other things) that some kind of national identity is desirable to reinforce our sense of – and commitment to – Australia as a society. The virtue of a "civil identity" is that it allows for "hyphenated identities" of the kind found in America with its Irish-Americans, Latino-Americans, Jewish-Americans, Muslim-Americans and so forth. The second part of these hyphenated identities, he thinks, is an identification with American society, the first part with a culture of origin, or with a religion. The important point is that Americans feel no less American for being also Polish, Italian, Christian, atheist etc. The conservatism is located, as it were, on the left-hand side of the hyphen, the liberalism on the right-hand side.

However, conservatism, whether taken as a tradition of thought or as a political tradition, does not have the resources to think through, or to realise, the kind of Australian citizenship Waleed Aly would like to see. For what would be the substance of the notion of civil identity? Again, Waleed Aly suggests we borrow from America, where the common identity of Americans as American is centred on the ideal of liberty. Leaving aside the fact that that ideal is unlikely to inspire in Australia, the lesson from America is precisely that this is *not* a unifying ideal. For America is deeply divided over what liberty means and, on one side at least, charges that the other side is "un-American" flow freely. More generally, it is doubtful that there is any single idea or ideal powerful enough to be the unifying focus of an Australian civil identity, which does not also have the potential for such divisive tendencies. An *ideal* could always be interpreted to support accusations that someone, or some group, is un-Australian. The conservative tradition, however, understands society as a spiritual or moral unity and so, to give substance to a notion of civil identity, it has only ideals of one kind or another to turn to. The idea of a "civil identity" is too valuable to be confined to the future of conservatism.

*

In essence, Waleed Aly's essay is an appeal to conservatives to be conservative about their tradition, to return to fundamental principles betrayed in the turn to neo-liberalism and neo-conservatism. As such, it resonates with the appeal to social democrats by the dying historian Tony Judt ("What Is Living and What Is Dead in Social Democracy," *New York Review of Books*, 17 December 2009). Judt asks social democrats to likewise eschew their decades-long embrace of neo-liberalism and to unashamedly defend both the idea, and much of the history, of the welfare state – that is, to return to *their* fundamentals. Despite the uncertain times in which we live, neither Waleed Aly or Tony Judt is seeking to develop, right now, any grand new political vision – in a manner always popular on the Left and now with red Tories planning to "transcend the dichotomy between the market state and the dysfunctional bureaucratic state." (The time of writing is two weeks before the British elections.) It is, I think, an admirable caution, and the stance adopted by Alexis de Tocqueville when he wrote, in times as "interesting" as our own:

> Yet this I own, that this old world, beyond which neither of us can see, appears to me to be almost worn out; the vast and venerable machine seems more out of gear every day; and though I cannot look forward, my faith in the continuance of the present is shaken. But it is no less the duty of honest men to stand up for the only system they understand. (July 1850)

Indeed, Judt's concluding plea could almost have been written by Waleed Aly:

> Rather than seeking to restore a language of optimistic progress, we should begin by reacquainting ourselves with the recent past. The first task of radical dissenters today is to remind their audience of the achievements of the twentieth century, along with the likely consequences of our heedless rush to dismantle them.

Almost. One change is required, namely the substitution of "nineteenth" for "twentieth" century. The conservative liberal achievements which Waleed Aly values belong mainly to the former, the welfare state to the latter. But what is striking is that these two patently "honest men" are nevertheless "standing up" for much the same kind of thing. When Judt maintains that society "still means something" and articulates that in terms of the social-democratic ideal of a people with "a willingness to pay for other people's services and benefits" because of "the understanding that they in turn will do likewise for you and your children: *because they are like you and see the world as you do*" (my italics), he is spelling out a vision very like that contained in Waleed Aly's notion of a civil identity, an understanding of citizens *qua* citizens and which unites people without encroaching on their differences. However, Judt does not fill out the perception that "others are like you and see the world as you do" in terms of common ideas or ideals. For him, such an understanding is contained in a shared willingness to contribute a portion of income to the common good. In the sense that it leaves our ideas and values untouched, his conception is more liberal than Waleed Aly's.

So construed, the social-democratic achievements of the twentieth century are not so much different from the conservative-liberal ideals of the nineteenth century, as their continuation. The social-democratic project was to provide the material, economic basis for a society which unites people, without interfering with their other life pursuits. The kind of liberalism Waleed Aly wants to restore is assumed – at least in principle. The point is a much stronger one than that the two traditions share similar ideals; it is that they require each other. In short, the future for Waleed Aly's kind of liberal conservatism is social-democratic.

*

In *The Conservative Mind*, Russell Kirk lists as one of the ten canons of conservatism that "conservatives know man to be governed more by emotion than by reason." Accordingly, conservatives understand politics to consist in an appeal more to emotion than to reason. And their favourite (political) emotion is fear. Fear is an acknowledgment of insecurity, of the fragility of the civilised edifice we have built. It cautions us against radical change and inhibits the angry or self-righteous impulses which draw people to oppositional movements. This is a dimension of conservative thought in which, ironically, Tony Judt grounds his argument, but which Waleed Aly bypasses. Were he to take it up and explore the possible emotional appeal of his idea of civic unity, he would find himself, I suggest, drawn even more strongly to social-democratic thinking. Moreover, without some such exploration, he is left in the contradictory position of appealing to conservatives on the basis of principle – the liberal principles they are in danger of forgetting – when the tradition eschews such politics of principle.

There is more than an appeal to principle in Tony Judt's polemic. His argument is for a "social democracy of fear," meaning that fear is the emotion which can encourage us to think again about the virtues of the welfare state. Our present global condition is one of insecurity, both economic and political. Social democrats, he maintains, would do well to emphasise that and to appeal, accordingly, to fear, emphasising how greater social security could modify these fears. And they would do well to remember that the post-war welfare state was grounded in fear: "the fear of a return to extremist politics, the politics of desperation, the politics of envy, the politics of fear." Fear, if unchecked, pits people against each other, but it can also be channelled, Judt thinks, to bring people together in mutual support. His is a very modern version of Hobbes's argument that fear is the most solid basis of a stable society – modern, because the solution to calming these fears is no longer submission to a powerful sovereign but the willingness to fund both a social infrastructure and social security. Judt's "social democracy of fear" would provide, then, the economic basis that would sustain a civil identity, and an understanding of how, in very general terms, this can be "pitched" politically.

Although Judt makes his case only by incorporating one of the canons of conservatism, this is something which can't be done with the resources of the conservative tradition as a tradition. Certainly, there is nothing in the conservative tradition which prevents it from addressing our present anxieties – on the contrary. But equally there is nothing in it which would enable it to meet these in a way which, at the same time, binds us together into a tolerant society. The standard conservative answer to economic insecurity is property – private property, make more people home-owners. However much this may appeal, it is clearly a solution which privatises, not socialises. And present fears, although in the first instance economic, are equally of the social unrest and fragmentation likely to ensue. The latter tend to be fears either of minority groups or fears for them – fears of their victimisation. The conservative tradition has available to it, then, only two ways of meeting these social fears. It can reinforce them in the hope of electoral success, or it can appeal to liberal principles of tolerance. The first is shameful, the second, which would amount to the "enlightened" middle class preaching to the "red-necks," ineffectual.

It is not, then, in the future of conservatism as a political movement that Waleed Aly will find the means to effectively promote an Australian civil identity. He could find it, though, in conservative ideas as utilised by the social-democratic tradition.

Jean Curthoys

WHAT'S RIGHT?

Correspondence

Martin Krygier

Waleed Aly has written a sparkling polemic in favour of conservatism and an older style of liberalism, and sharply critical of tendencies that, flying under false colours, appear to have usurped the labels but not the wisdom or the insights that informed them.

I share Aly's taste for conservative and liberal thought, and admire his sympathetic and textured appreciation of them. I also share his distaste for much of the dogmatic free-floating universalism, and complexity-and-culture-reducing individualism, that so often drive what has come to be known as neo-liberal thought. So too for the put 'em up, shoot (or shout) 'em down style that has come to characterise what passes for conservatism in recent years. The two neos are characterised as much by what they exclude as what they include; in fact, exclusion is often what it's all about in the "trench warfare" that, as Aly laments, substitutes for public discussion in this country. To reject a view because it does "not side with the right 'team,'" as Aly puts it, is a negative form of what philosophers expose as an "argument from authority" (rather than evidence and logic), and it is spurious wherever you find it.

Yet it appears hard to teach even a young (and smart) dog new tricks, and I fear that Aly falls for some old ones. Indeed, precisely those that he rightly warns us against. For once the world of political ideas is aligned – conservative/liberal (socialist is rarely mentioned) *versus* neo-conservative/neo-liberal – it is not clear we have left the trenches very far behind. As Andrew Kenny observes in the article Aly begins with and rightly commends, "There seems to be some inherent flaw in the human brain that encourages people to fissure into two groups who loathe each other. Almost any argument in politics, religion or science soon results in two warring parties accusing each other of heresy, apostasy, false belief, treachery and being rotters. This is destructive to progress and knowledge." Aly, of course, knows this, but it is a misstep he doesn't always avoid, particularly in the latter parts of his essay.

Often the weightiest, and certainly the most common, argument Aly musters against all those neos he combats is that they are not really conservative. That is an intramural point worth making, since that is what they call themselves. However, a bigger point than whether a position is conservative is whether it is right or helps us get things right, in the pre-1789 sense of the word. If that is presumed to follow automatically from staying in or leaving the camp to which one belongs, then we are back in those trenches again.

Perhaps that wouldn't matter if we could be sure that the con/libs had all the answers and the neos none of them, or that the best answers might not escape all the combatants we have arrayed. But, and it's an old conservative truth, we can never be sure of that.

Take conservatism itself. Aly warmly and deftly points to the sense of complexity, the presumption in favour of traditions and what exists, the allergy to hubris in politics, the respect for what has been tried and found, for whatever reason, adequate, that the conservative disposition wisely commends. It is progressivist folly to imagine we ever can start with a clean slate or that we're smart enough to do whatever we want with the one that history presents to us. However, slates can be disgustingly dirty or have dirty corners which need to be – though it's hard – wiped clean. Conservatives are not always the best at pointing that out, or doing much about it.

For conservatism has two characteristic strands. One commends a particular way of thinking and acting appropriate to public affairs; call this methodological. The other expresses an attachment to familiar features of the society in which the conservative lives, features they worry might be threatened. This might be called normative conservatism.

The lessons of methodological conservatism are well-nigh universal: the world is complex; radical change will always have unintended effects, often unwelcome; things that have lasted a decent time are likely to have something going for them, or at any rate are likely to be pretty sticky; you're not that smart, where the "you" in question is quite unspecific. These lessons need to be heeded whether you like what exists or not. You will never do well to ignore it, even if you want to change it.

The virtues of normative conservatism are more variable. When Michael Oakeshott recommended the pursuit of the intimations of traditions, rather than rationalist programs of reform, it helped that he was fond of both the traditions and their intimations. What if deeply embedded traditions are lousy, as they often are? Their intimations aren't likely to be very different. Methodological conservatism still makes sense: it's never smart to ignore the specifics of what is going on around you, indeed often inside you, and has been there for some time. They're likely to bite you, whatever you think of them. But do you have to like them? Sometimes the best people don't and the worst do. Normative conservatism, however, doesn't automatically discriminate. Liberalism does allow for better discrimination, but often it does so in direct competition with its conservative partner. Even in the best case, liberalism being a "progressive" mode of thought and conservatism often highly suspicious of progress, there are many tensions in this marriage, perhaps more than Aly concedes.

That is true even where liberalism is strong. It is all the more so elsewhere. Aly rightly concentrates on the British "rather than the Russian" conservative tradition but he knows that "ideas cannot be neatly contained by national borders and often have to be discussed in broad terms." And if we move to Russia, Vladimir Putin appears to be a rather doughty normative conservative who, like those Aly invokes, knows that "established institutions are to be cherished and preserved." Taking Aly's point, he might be heard to say, "None of that Anglo-nonsense about rights, property, the rule of law, restraint on central power. That's no part of *our* tradition. *Nyet* to all that!" What are we to say to Russians (or Iranians) who are dismayed by such conservatism?

Of course, such a response doesn't flow inevitably from conservatism; few things flow inevitably from rich and complex traditions. However, it is an available option and it has often been taken. And if we move back to Britain, recall Tom Paine's complaint that in his remarkable *Reflections on the Revolution in France*, Burke "pities the plumage and forgets the dying bird." Paine might have exaggerated and even if not, Burke is a giant of political intelligence and, more than intelligence, wisdom. Yet Paine has a point, and it is not an answer (though true) to rebut him by saying, as Aly does of American rhetoric, that "it is about as far away from Burke as you can get."

There is another problem with too much dichotomising in the world of ideas. It is not only that the sources of guidance must always be found within the team to which one belongs. Once the world of ideas is carved up this way, if something goes wrong it seems natural, inevitable, that your enemy is behind it. And so it is hard to know what *not* to blame the neos for. I have a general and a specific concern here.

The general one is that many of the modern pathologies of which Aly writes can plausibly be traced to structures, technologies and embedded "hardware" of the development of modern and now hyper-modern societies, not to mention "software" – ideas and ideals – that have developed in dramatic and world-transforming ways over the past couple of centuries. Marx was not always wrong, nor Weber, when they pointed to the many strains and corrosions (and also extraordinary possibilities) that have attended post-eighteenth century modernity. The modern world, not just its present hyper-incarnation, *is* different from anything else. Not wholly, else conservatism would have no purchase, but deeply.

One catastrophic difference we are now threatened with is global warming, but since that is a development of the industrial age, its *genesis* owes nothing to neo-libs or neo-cons. On this reading of contemporary (by which I mean the last 200 years) developments, the mistake of neo-liberals is that they endorse those developments so heartily that they have no resources or will to apply any brakes. That can be a terrible failing but it is not the same as *causing* the pathologies, many of which would have challenged any political order and its thinkers, whatever their ideological conformation.

Secondly, once an all-purpose accusatory label gets moving, there is nowhere it won't go. Take Bulgaria, for example, as indeed Aly does. Perhaps it is not fair to place too much weight on what he says about it, since it does not appear to be his special field, but there is a symptomatic quality to what he does say, which is meant to travel far beyond the benighted Balkans.

Bulgaria is Aly's representation of post-communism as afflicted by Western neo-liberalism, which is put upon it but doesn't suit it. There are several elements in the charge. First, Bulgarians are unhappy (as, by the way, they have often been and had reason to be). It is not clear that all post-communists are unhappy, or as unhappy as Bulgarians. It would have made a difference if he had begun elsewhere, say Poland, or looked at just how much things vary among and within countries of the region, and how much has changed immeasurably for the better in so many parts of the post-communist world. Communism was arguably, but of course not really, one story; post-communism is unarguably many.

Secondly, this is alleged all to be a product of a program by "Western elites, many of whom were conservative politicians, [who, after the collapse of communism] immediately set about remaking the world in accordance with one version of the neo-liberal dream, starting with the former communist states." Note that local elites, structures, people, traditions, customs, don't rate a mention, even though, as every conservative knows, they are central to the sticky stuff of societies, and as conservatives often have warned, it is folly to assume them all away when you try to push other countries around in order to "remake the world." Sometimes they become flies in your ointment, even cockroaches in your soup, to use a distinction recently made by Avishai Margalit. What comes out of even the most meticulously planned concoctions has a heavily local taste.

Thirdly, these elites are said to have ignored what every conservative knows: "that the free market works best when it has evolved naturally from the culture and institutions of the society in which it exists." What is the implication here? Is it that reform should skip Bulgaria, that since Bulgaria and every other communist country had endured for forty to seventy years a phenomenally destructive "Caesaro-Papist-Mammonist" order, otherwise known as communism, it should continue to do so, because nothing else could suit them? Shouldn't these elites have realised that "an inorganic, externally constructed, global political revolution on neo-liberal lines was a project fraught with difficulty"? It might surprise Aly, but a lot of people in the post-communist region have suspected this for some time, since 1989 in fact, when to everyone's surprise the geopolitical map of the world was transformed and the question was not what to do when you have all the options, but rather how to respond to the only circumstances you have, viz., the ones you're in. It is no doubt true that "the most successful nations have been those where existing social and political forces were favourable to economic reform." You don't need to be a conservative, or anything really, to believe that. But where does that leave Bulgaria and many other countries which happen not to be the most prominent among those, after that preposterous regime had imploded but certainly not disappeared, strewing its traces and legacies everywhere? Sometimes the disease is actually worse than the cure.

This leads to the deepest misconception of all in Aly's analysis, one that he shares with the more optimistic interveners he attacks: that what has happened in Sofia, or Bucharest, or Zagreb etc., and I haven't even left the Balkans, is all a result of some unrelenting application of neo-liberal policies by Western elites. However, as Venelin Ganev, a friend of Ivan Krastev's (on whom Aly relies) and of mine, and one of the leading writers on Bulgaria and post-communism generally, argues powerfully (in his *Preying on the State: The Transformation of Bulgaria after 1989*), "policy-centered" explanations of post-communist developments, central among them attribution of the fate of the region to neo-liberalism, "suffer from several serious defects: factual inaccuracy, neglect of historical and institutional context, and implausible assumptions about elite behaviour." More specifically, he explains that during the first half-dozen years of post-communism, when key reforms were instituted, outside the contentious case of Russia the only country in the region "where a handful of intellectuals who had actually read Friedrich Hayek and embraced his ideas about the state and the market enjoyed their fifteen minutes of fame" was Poland, and even there Polish neo-liberals had and have their hands full resisting nationalists, Catholics and others to whom Hayek and co. are anathema. Normative conservatism, however and sometimes alas, is not. Poland was, he shows, the exception not the rule, and one might add that it's a rather inconvenient one for those who would blame neo-liberalism for post-communist problems, since Poland's post-communist two decades lead the field by some way.

Ganev rejects the common default assumption that neo-liberalism caused and explains whatever went badly after communism. He argues powerfully that dysfunctional structures and legacies of local ex-communist states, which did not just curl up and die in 1989, and the predatory opportunities and resources available to local elites, were far more significant than neo-liberal policies in the new post-communist circumstances. The moral of this story has elsewhere been drawn by Ganev: "it would be nice if we lived in a mono-diabolical world, where isolating Satan in a single 'shooting-chamber' and taking him down would have been easy. Alas, it turns out that problems in various parts of the world are due to different causes, and blanket denunciation of 'neo-liberalism' contributes nothing to our understanding of what is happening and why." I mention this not to defend neo-liberals. Let them do it; for many reasons, among them Aly's, I am not a fan (nor is Ganev). However, nor am I fond of the sort of simplifying lumping that even a thinker of Aly's sophistication is drawn to in order to clarify who's who in the world, and – perhaps more to the point – who's to blame.

Some years ago, I sought to extend the inspiration of the great Polish philosopher Leszek Kołakowski. He had written a credo for a "conservative-liberal-socialist International," since he believed that, despite their differences, each of these major traditions contained important truths that were consistent and could be combined. Though he warned that his "great and powerful International … will never exist, because it cannot promise people that they will be happy," he argued persuasively that it made sense. In the conviction that Kołakowski was right but too modest, I proposed a more ambitious venture, the "conservative-liberal-republican-communitarian-social-democratic" International. I don't believe that his International has many members, and mine has just one to my knowledge. But I'm not giving up. I'm hoping for Aly.

All of us, and especially his neo-targets, need to take his thoughtful and powerful argument, and the traditions that he recovers with such sympathy and intelligence, with the greatest seriousness. One way of doing that is to avoid the conceit that those in the opposing trench are the source of all your problems. No conservative liberal should believe that, and nor should anyone else.

Martin Krygier

WHAT'S
RIGHT?

Response to
Correspondence

Waleed Aly

I struggle with the concept of progressive conservatism. In the terms employed in my essay, it is a contradiction: progressivism and conservatism are polar opposites. Nonetheless, it has turned out to be one of the year's more important political ideas. David Cameron, for one, is a believer. In January 2009 he launched the Progressive Conservatism Project at Demos, a London think-tank, where he outlined his vision:

> First, a society that is fair, where we help people out of poverty and help them stay out of it – for life. Second, a society where opportunity is equal, where everyone can, in Michael Gove's brilliant phrase, "write their own life-story." Third, a society that is greener, where we pass on a planet that is environmentally sustainable, clean and beautiful to future generations. And fourth, a safer society, where people are protected from threat and fear.

That, it has to be said, does have a progressive resonance. It holds up a model society that it seeks to achieve. But, as Cameron argues the case, these objectives are best achieved through what he calls "conservative means": decentralisation of power, government action to strengthen the institutions of civil society, economic growth and a government that lives within its means. It is doubtful that economic growth can be claimed for conservatism in this way, but otherwise he has a point.

What is immediately striking about Cameron's vision is how distant it is from Thatcherism. "There is such a thing as society," boomed the Conservatives' manifesto for the 2010 election, pointedly. Cameron seems to have taken his philosophical inspiration from Phillip Blond, the self-described Red Tory, whose dislike of Thatcher's politics is well known. Blond, in turn, takes his inspiration from the Middle Ages, where he sees small, localised, self-sufficient communities, unhampered by an invasive central state and secure from the ravages of a monstrous, alienating global economy. Here is the progressive-conservative alternative to neo-liberalism: not simply a small state, but a "big society."

Society has become something of a preoccupation for Britain's Conservative Party. Take Iain Duncan Smith, not long ago an ardent defender of the neo-liberal project, who has since turned to fixing what he calls Britain's "broken society." Hayek would be livid: Duncan Smith even went on to establish the Centre for Social Justice. He's not talking markets anymore. He's talking traditional family values. Cameron, meanwhile, is talking compassionate capitalism. In Hayekian terms, that makes little sense.

Truth be told, the Tories should be devastated with their showing at last month's election. Yes, they won a historic swing and ultimately the prime ministership, but consider the facts. Labour had been in power for thirteen years. Its leader had few charismatic gifts and no strong record of prime ministerial achievement. Britain had just been through an awful recession. That the Conservatives could not win an outright majority in these circumstances suggests that there is something repellent about the Tory brand. Victory should have been foolproof. As it happened, the result was heavily compromised and decidedly tricky.

Does that mean the end for progressive conservatism? That depends more than a little on how one reads the Tories' failure. Cameron's green enthusiasm of 2009, rather like Kevin Rudd's, seems to have been diluted considerably through 2010. The rigours of the election campaign and the dire state of Britain's economy forced Cameron to talk repeatedly about the need to limit public spending. That had him sounding less like the David Cameron of a year ago and more like the Iron Lady. Do we interpret the result as a rejection of Red Toryism, or rather as evidence of a reluctance on the electorate's part to believe the Conservatives have truly moved on from Thatcherism?

Jean Curthoys is right to distinguish the thoughts in my essay from the Blond/Cameron brand of progressive conservatism. As she perceptively notes, Cameron's big society would require the state to re-create the communities on which it is founded. The world has moved on since the Middle Ages, and there strikes me as little that is truly organic in this new vision. My fear is that Blond's views suffer from a similar (though perhaps less odious) tinge of nostalgia as that which I criticised in neo-conservatism. No doubt Blond would have answers to that charge. After all, he calls for a modern expression of the best features of medieval society, which is not quite the same thing as the retrieval of an imagined history.

Still, I would require more convincing that this kind of conservatism would not ultimately succumb to its progressivism.

I must apologise to Martin Krygier for continuing with such a binary. Krygier sees in my essay a continued (if altered) form of the very trench warfare I began the piece by deriding. Let me say immediately that if there is to be trench warfare, then I would much rather it be waged in the realm of ideas (such as liberal-conservative versus neo-liberal neo-conservative) than on the basis of meaningless teams (such as Left and Right). But in any case, I feel a clarification is in order. I don't require the world to be conservative, liberal or anything else particularly. I confess to a sympathy for much conservative political philosophy, and I am suspicious of many progressive political programs, but that is not to say the world would always be better off without them. The most obvious and powerful criticism of conservatism, one noted by Krygier and in my essay, is that it is often blind to circumstances where tradition is oppressive. What, for instance, would conservatism have had to say of apartheid South Africa? What was the appropriate conservative position on the abolition of slavery in the United States, and was Abraham Lincoln, a Republican president, a conservative? Confronted with such situations, I hope I would be more progressive than conservative. Ideally, the conservative's allergy to dogma means she is compelled to appreciate the contribution of progressive political ideas, even as she opposes them. My analysis is not intended to rest, as Krygier seems to suggest, on any assertion that liberal-conservatives hold all the answers and "the neos" none of them. Nor do I believe every evil in the world can be traced to "neo" ideologies.

For instance, I fear Krygier reads too much into my discussion of post-communist Bulgaria. I happily acknowledge (and indeed acknowledged) that the assessment of post-communist societies' success is complex and ongoing. I certainly do not assert that economic liberalisation has been an unmitigated disaster. I argue that the mixed results sit uncomfortably with neo-liberalism's universalist, quasi-utopian claims manifest in a thirst for shock therapy and predictions of the end of history. It is unnecessary to demonstrate that neo-liberalism is the cause of all the post-communist world's ills – clearly, it isn't – in order to hold that the facts equally rebut the progressivist ambitions of neo-liberal thought.

Similarly, I have not argued that neo-liberalism caused the financial crisis, as Tom Switzer charges. I think there is probably a strong argument to that effect, but I also said explicitly that there might be a plausible argument to the contrary. In my essay I quite deliberately do not take a position on the issue and say that it is a debate best left to better economic minds than mine.

I do not believe (or assert) that climate change's genesis lies in neo-liberalism, as Krygier alleges. It has more to do with the industrial revolution. I argue merely that climate change presents an intractable ideological problem for neo-liberals because it requires us to subordinate market rationality to something else. That is to say, I agree entirely with Krygier to the extent that he believes "the mistake of neo-liberals is that they endorse those developments so heartily that they have no resources or will to apply any brakes." Obviously, Andrew Norton objects to that characterisation, citing his own online survey of ideological opinion on climate change, where respondents who supported the free market were more likely to support action than those who selected other labels to describe themselves, such as "conservative." The problem is that my analysis is not ultimately about self-description, but about ideological commitment. John Howard, for instance, described himself as conservative. I have argued he isn't. Norton is free to dispute that categorisation (he is silent on it), but it underscores the fact that the label someone uses to describe themselves in an online survey does not necessarily have any relationship to the terms used in my essay. Within the context of the survey, I really have no idea what "conservative" means. Nor do I know what "classical liberal" means in the mind of the respondent. I have no doubt that there are many people who both believe in a free market and who are very supportive of climate-change action. That is borne out by the fact that not a few entrepreneurs and business people were more supportive of the emissions trading scheme than the Liberal Party turned out to be.

My arguments on climate change were focused on the impact of neo-liberal ideas on politics, not on business people or survey respondents. And here, I believe, the record is revealing. In lists of conservative leaders who have taken climate change most seriously (and contrary to Switzer's assertions, I have not argued all self-described conservatives are denialists), Angela Merkel, Nicolas Sarkozy and David Cameron are most often cited. Of course, these leaders can hardly be described as neo-liberal. Cameron's divergences from neo-liberalism have already been noted. Merkel's Christian Democrats are not Germany's neo-liberal party – the Free Democratic Party is, and only last year did it work its way into Merkel's governing coalition. Sarkozy may be as close to a neo-liberal leader as France has had, but he could scarcely pass for a neo-liberal in the Anglosphere. By contrast, some of the strongest strains of climate scepticism among conservative parties (aside from Australia) seem to be found in the United States, where the Republicans have held passionately to their neo-liberal convictions. Then, of course, for colour we might add the Czech Republic, whose president, Václav Klaus, is ardently neo-liberal and must surely be the most hardened climate-change denier among world leaders. Anyone looking for the quintessential case of conspiratorial climate-change denialism in action should read his speech in 2008 to the neo-liberal Mont Pelerin Society.

Yes, there are some counter-examples. New Zealand's John Key is one. The most powerful is undoubtedly Margaret Thatcher. They suggest that neo-liberalism's blindness to environmental destruction is not absolute in practice, and I am prepared to accept such a modification of my argument, but they do not disrupt the correlation that has by now become clear. Even if Norton is right that the concept of "negative externalities" equips neo-liberalism with the capacity to respond to environmental degradation (and that is a complex discussion), it nonetheless remains true that those with neo-liberal inclinations are often the least disposed to "internalising" such "externalities."

What, then, should the conservative response to climate change be? I have not sought to answer that question, except to say that conservatives should accept the reality of the problem. Here Switzer protests, deeming climate change a "speculative problem" whose solutions "would lead to radical and disruptive changes that in turn could have a substantial and detrimental impact on the lives of the Australian people." "What if the Cassandras are wrong or have seriously exaggerated the threat?" he asks, to which the most obvious answer is: and what if the scientists are right – on a scientific issue? Switzer's approach is really to bet. He is honest enough not to claim the scientific ability to determine the issue for himself, nor does he make the argument, so far as I can tell, that he has the weight of scientific opinion on his side. He argues simply that scientists have been wrong in the past and might be so again. The question for present purposes, I suppose, is whether such scepticism is conservative. Perhaps so, if it is conservative to be suspicious of science. I understand the conservative suspicion of grand theories and ideological programs, but I'm not convinced that requires a rejection of the best scientific knowledge available simply because it has grave implications. Of course, it is entirely Switzer's choice to take this gamble. I'm just not sure it is conservatism's best hope for the future.

That said, there is something important in Switzer's response. If the scientists are right, climate change presents a radical challenge to our world. Does the conservative take the pragmatic course of facing up to the reality of the problem, or does the conservative resist action on the basis that any such action will of necessity be radically disruptive? The best conservative option would be to find a solution that is not unduly disruptive – and here I would like to hear more of Switzer's ideas on adaptation. I disagree with his assertion that an emissions trading scheme is necessarily radical, but I do have reservations about its effectiveness. It is an important point, though, because if no smooth solution exists, a very real question is raised about whether or not conservatism has much to say in response to this issue.

Conservatism, however, should have something to say on society. Norton rejects my argument that neo-liberalism subordinates social values to market imperatives because "prior to [exchange] must be the values set by individuals. Culture, sentiment and ethics can all give things a value above money, blocking any exchange." That is all true enough, but it implies an artificially static view of the market's operation. Markets, in fact, are dynamic and have a structural power of their own. They are not mere conduits for the expression of human sentiment. They set in motion forces that *shape* such sentiment. Advertising, for instance, transmits a system of values to the consumer, one that the advertiser hopes makes the consumer more likely to buy their product. The political problem caused by a conception of society that is held together by relations that, in Hayek's phrase, are purely "economic," is that one can ultimately find a market in just about anything. Child trafficking for prostitution, for instance, feeds a market. Clearly the participants in that market have no values-driven barrier to its existence. The political question, however, is whether or not such a market should be allowed to exist. That is a value judgment that comes from beyond the market in question. In an extreme example such as that, the answer may appear simple, but things get trickier in less brutal cases. That is why I raised the example of the sexualisation of children in advertising and commerce, or corporate paedophilia. Clearly, a market exists for such sexualisation. Clearly, therefore, it expresses the values of certain people. But it does more than that. It also shapes them by promoting and normalising a particular system of values. Moreover it is promoted by powerful social actors, such as corporations. Should it be allowed to flourish unchecked? That is a political judgment that cannot be determined satisfactorily by leaving the outcome to market mechanisms.

"The arts, the entertainment industry and the media" are also in the habit of "pushing the boundaries with the sexualisation of children," writes John Hirst in his response, making the point that business is not alone in doing this. Let us leave aside for the moment that Hirst serenely ignores the fact that the media and entertainment industries *are* businesses and may safely be assumed to be following market imperatives very often. His point, that the sexualisation of children is more than merely a market phenomenon, is entirely valid. Unfortunately, it has little to do with my argument. I raised the subject of the sexualisation of children not to label it a result of neo-liberalism but to demonstrate that a conservative in neo-liberalism's thrall has no response to it. And while it is easy to see the neo-liberal argument in defence of corporate paedophilia, what business does a conservative have in making such an argument? In my estimation, none.

And so, to return to Krygier, the point here is not to blame "the neos" for every malady. I have little positive to say about neo-conservatism, it is true. But I could easily nominate some benefits of neo-liberalism, even non-economic ones. For instance, in promoting the individual, and individual choice, it has contributed to a more interesting, diverse and generally tolerant society. But none of that changes the fact – more or less conceded by Switzer – that it is a radically transformative force. That makes it an un-conservative one. My interest was to examine the way conservatism is compromised by signing up to such progressive political projects.

In the case of neo-conservatism, and perhaps of progressive conservatism, the result is a kind of nostalgia. Blond wants to re-conceive of society in localised, even parochial terms, while neo-conservatives want to limit social membership to those who share, or at least do not threaten, their view of the world. I have floated the idea of a civilly constituted society because I believe it is more in tune with our present circumstances and does not succumb to nostalgia.

George Brandis, while accepting several of my criticisms of Howard's cultural politics, rejects my attempts to call it neo-conservative. For Brandis, Howard was genuinely conservative to the extent that he emphasised the importance of social cohesion. Were that the end of the matter, it would be hard to argue. No doubt social cohesion is a perfectly respectable conservative concern. Still, after considering Brandis's argument, I cannot bring myself to describe Howard's approach to social cohesion as conservative. As Brandis himself acknowledges, Howard's self-declared appropriation of the mainstream made for a socially *divisive* discourse. Only if you assume, for instance, that Asians are not part of our society can you describe Howard's awful, prolonged silence on the substance of Hansonism as promoting cohesion. It is difficult to resist the conclusion that Howard was either genuinely blind to the inclusion of Asian-Australians as part of our society, or that the only social cohesion with which he was concerned was that of a sub-set of the Australian population of largely Anglo-Celtic extraction.

Of course, Howard would never express it so crudely. He is on the record as being proud of a multiracial Australia as long as it isn't multicultural. That is a monocultural view, and it is not rendered otherwise by noting, as Brandis does, that Howard ran record levels of non-European migration. Indeed, this merely allows us to discern Howard's social un-conservatism. A multiracial, monocultural society can only exist on the assumption that such factors as race, ethnicity, religion and culture can neatly be cleaved from one another. No conservative should believe that – at least not if they are remotely familiar with conservatism's considerable insights into human nature. We are historical, relational, memorial beings. People do not simply adopt cultural modes of thought and behaviour once lectured sufficiently to do so. In fact, incessant lecturing is likely only to inspire stubborn resistance. In the case of Australian Muslims, the effect of Howard's Australianness ultimatum was to make large numbers of them feel less Australian, more marginalised, less patriotic and less integrated. That is to say, it made our society less cohesive – and any conservative should have been able to predict that.

Assimilationism – and I am comfortable using that word to describe Howard's approach – is a *progressive* ideal, not a conservative one. It is an idea that accords with the French Revolution, which is precisely why it remains so vividly present in French social politics. It is for this reason that I believe conservatives should consider the virtues of a civil national identity. To be clear, I am not arguing that civil identities are inherently superior to cultural ones in all circumstances. In fact, I don't believe they are: Europe's cultural richness appeals to me more than America's in this sense. But I also believe that Europe's age has passed. Our hyper-globalised world – created in no small part by neo-liberalism – renders national identity based on shared culture a nostalgic anachronism that is destined to be repressive. This is a problem that similarly threatens to bedevil the localised communities Blond and Cameron so desire. The conservative is perfectly entitled to bemoan that fact, but not to deny it or seek refuge in some nostalgic brand of cultural fundamentalism. In our current circumstances, a civil conception of national identity strikes me as the most pragmatic response. It takes account of the prevailing circumstances and of human nature. To respond to Curthoys, therein lies its conservatism.

Precisely what form that civil identity might take is an open question. In the United States, the uniting value is individual liberty, but I take on board the retorts of Curthoys and Hirst that this may not work for Australia. I suspect the attachment of Australian citizens to the concept of liberty may be underestimated, but even if not, my argument remains. Perhaps equality or egalitarianism is a more natural fit. Perhaps some other civic value is appropriate. I consider it to be entirely within our grasp to find a civic expression of ourselves. This, as much as anything, is a function of how our leaders respond to emerging social phenomena. Do they take their cues from Howard's approach to Muslims, or to the Exclusive Brethren? Each sets in motion a different social conversation, and with it, over time, a different perception of ourselves as a nation. I am simply arguing that if we wish a radically (and irreversibly) plural nation such as ours to cohere, we should value things like citizenship, rather than have a view of citizenship that is contingent on an approved set of values.

That may be a little too much Mill for Hirst, who resorts quickly to the spectre of "Islamic separatism." How can we be cutely concerned about the niceties of pluralism when young Muslims want to blow us up? Hirst's urging echoes the neo-conservative cultural orthodoxy and falls for its traps. Hirst is right to be concerned about the threat, which I do not question, and indeed spend considerable amounts of time trying to analyse. But in advancing such an argument, he surprises me by missing several fundamental points. Yes, Islamist radicalism is real, but exactly how is it addressed by lecturing Muslims on integration? It isn't, but Hirst simply assumes that it is. In fact, the problem is more likely to be exacerbated by this, as it makes Muslims with no radical designs at all increasingly alienated from the national mythology. Hirst is offensively wrong to suggest that the London bombers do not worry me. They do, and it is precisely because they worry me that I find neo-conservatism's narrowness and belligerence so wrong-headed. I have seen the alienation it causes first-hand, and it should make Hirst far less comfortable and relaxed than anything I have written.

But of course, the most fundamental point that Hirst ignores is about collectivism. My essay argued that neo-conservatism's monoculturalist discourse violated the liberal-conservative tradition's preference for allowing people their individuality. If Hirst's response to Islamist radicalism is to support the lecturing of Muslims on values, he merely embraces – and abets – that false collectivism. Yes, about two dozen Australian Muslims have been arrested on terrorism charges. That, in no small part, is due to the efforts of other Australian Muslims who provided intelligence to the authorities. And then there are the hundreds of thousands of others who had no intelligence to provide because the whole phenomenon has almost nothing to do with their lives. Should all these people be considered as though they are some undifferentiated mass by the very same people who claim to champion the autonomy of the individual? Yes, as Hirst notes, I do argue that identity is becoming increasingly de-territorialised. But that does not permit us to form a crudely collectivist view of our societies in the neo-conservative fashion. I did not devote much energy to the threat of home-grown terrorism in my essay, mainly because it was beside the points under discussion. That Hirst fails to see this only demonstrates the pitfalls and crudeness of neo-conservative thinking.

What, then, is the future of conservatism? The more I am forced to think about this, the more my mind turns to a more fundamental question raised briefly in my essay: does conservatism *have* a future? Switzer reads my essay as "pedd[ling] a pessimistic outlook for right-of-centre political parties, most notably Australia's Liberal Party." He is right to detect my pessimism, but he mischaracterises my target. To be honest, I don't have a particularly strong view on the electoral fate of such parties. I am, however, concerned about the future of conservatism as an intellectual and philosophical tradition. The parties Switzer calls "right-of-centre" may well be successful into the future. That doesn't mean they will be particularly conservative. In fact, it might mean the opposite.

My pessimism arises from the fact that ours is now a radical world. It is in a state of ever-increasing flux, of radical and irreversible pluralism and of impossibly complex and multiple identities. The political problems of the day – and climate change is only one example – seem to demand radical thought and responses that are alien to the conservative temperament. Perhaps, then, conservatism as a philosophical and intellectual tradition must simply bid farewell to a world that, partly by ignoring it, has left it in an impossible position. Or perhaps some great conservative thinker can revive it without resorting to nostalgia, belligerence or denial. And as for Krygier's "conservative-liberal-republican-communitarian-social-democratic" International, I'm all ears.

Waleed Aly

Waleed Aly is a lecturer in politics at Monash University. He is a regular commentator for the *Guardian*, the *Australian*, the *Australian Financial Review*, the *Sydney Morning Herald* and the *Age*, as well as ABC Melbourne radio and SBS's *Salam Café*. His book *People Like Us: How Arrogance Is Dividing Islam and the West* was published in 2007.

George Brandis is the deputy leader of the Opposition in the Senate. Before entering parliament he worked as a barrister and university lecturer, and co-edited two books on liberalism, *Liberals Face the Future: Essays on Australian Liberalism* (1984) and *Australian Liberalism: The Continuing Vision* (1986).

Jean Curthoys is a research associate with the School of Philosophy at the University of Sydney and the author of *Feminist Amnesia: The Wake of Women's Liberation* (1997). She is currently working on the social and philosophical origins of neo-liberalism as well as a new approach to English grammar.

John Hirst's recent books include *The Shortest History of Europe* (2009), *Freedom on the Fatal Shore* (2008), *Sense & Nonsense in Australian History* (2005) and a forthcoming collection of essays, *Looking for Australia*. Until recently he was reader in history at La Trobe University in Melbourne.

Martin Krygier is professor of law and co-director of the European Law Centre at the University of New South Wales. In 1997 he delivered the ABC's Boyer Lectures, "Between Fear and Hope: Hybrid Thoughts on Public Values." He is the author of *Civil Passions: Selected Writings* (2005).

David Marr is the multi-award-winning author of *Patrick White: A Life* and *The High Price of Heaven*, and co-author with Marian Wilkinson of *Dark Victory*. In a career spanning over thirty years, he has written for the *Bulletin* and the *Sydney Morning Herald*, been editor of the *National Times*, a reporter for *Four Corners* and presenter of ABC-TV's *Media Watch*. In 2007 he authored Quarterly Essay 26, *His Master's Voice*.

George Megalogenis is a senior journalist with the *Australian*, having spent eleven years in the Canberra press gallery between 1988 and 1999. He is the author of *Faultlines* (2003) and *The Longest Decade* (2006) and a regular panellist on ABC TV's *Insiders*.

Andrew Norton is editor of *Policy*, published by the Centre for Independent Studies. In 1993, he co-edited *A Defence of Economic Rationalism*. The results of his survey of ideological political opinion were published in the Spring 2009 issue of *Policy*, available at <www.policymagazine.com>.

Tom Switzer is a research associate at the United States Studies Centre at the University of Sydney. A former opinion editor of the *Australian* and Liberal pre-selection candidate for the federal seat of Bradfield, he is the editor of the *Spectator*'s Australian edition.

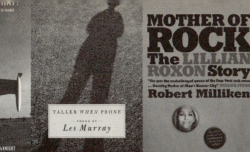

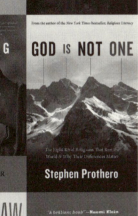
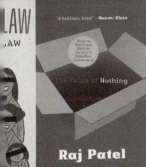
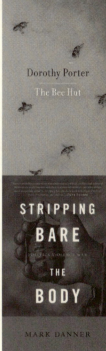
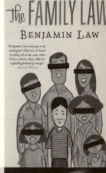

WIN A YEAR'S WORTH OF BOOKS!

SUBSCRIBE to *Quarterly Essay* today and go into the draw to win every book Black Inc. published between July 2009 and June 2010.*

That's 35 books up for grabs, including *Piano Lessons* by Anna Goldsworthy, *The Shortest History of Europe* by John Hirst, *The Value of Nothing* by Raj Patel, *Trouble* by Kate Jennings, and many more.

Subscribe to *Quarterly Essay* for only

$49 for a 1-year subscription
$95 for a 2-year subscription

& your bookcase could be full of fabulous new books.

Subscribe online at **www.quarterlyessay.com**

----

* Competition runs from 1 June 2010 – 31 July 2010. Competition open to new and renewing subscribers. Renewing subscribers receive standard renewal rates: $39 (1 year), $78 (2 years).

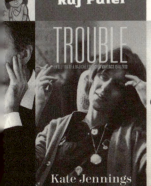
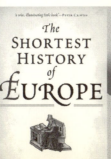

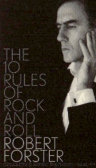

Subscribe to QUARTERLY ESSAY

Subscribe to Quarterly Essay and save 50% off the cover price

Subscriptions Receive a discount and never miss an issue. Mailed direct to your door.

- ☐ **1 year subscription** (4 issues): $49 a year within Australia incl. GST. Outside Australia $79.
- ☐ **2 year subscription** (8 issues): $95 a year within Australia incl. GST. Outside Australia $155.

* All prices include postage and handling.

Back Issues (Prices include postage and handling.)

- ☐ **QE 1** ($10.95) Robert Manne *In Denial*
- ☐ **QE 2** ($10.95) John Birmingham *Appeasing Jakarta*
- ☐ **QE 4** ($10.95) Don Watson *Rabbit Syndrome*
- ☐ **QE 5** ($12.95) Mungo MacCallum *Girt by Sea*
- ☐ **QE 6** ($12.95) John Button *Beyond Belief*
- ☐ **QE 7** ($12.95) John Martinkus *Paradise Betrayed*
- ☐ **QE 8** ($12.95) Amanda Lohrey *Groundswell*
- ☐ **QE 10** ($13.95) Gideon Haigh *Bad Company*
- ☐ **QE 11** ($13.95) Germaine Greer *Whitefella Jump Up*
- ☐ **QE 12** ($13.95) David Malouf *Made in England*
- ☐ **QE 13** ($13.95) Robert Manne with David Corlett *Sending Them Home*
- ☐ **QE 14** ($14.95) Paul McGeough *Mission Impossible*
- ☐ **QE 15** ($14.95) Margaret Simons *Latham's World*
- ☐ **QE 16** ($14.95) Raimond Gaita *Breach of Trust*
- ☐ **QE 17** ($14.95) John Hirst *"Kangaroo Court"*
- ☐ **QE 18** ($14.95) Gail Bell *The Worried Well*
- ☐ **QE 19** ($15.95) Judith Brett *Relaxed & Comfortable*
- ☐ **QE 20** ($15.95) John Birmingham *A Time for War*
- ☐ **QE 21** ($15.95) Clive Hamilton *What's Left?*
- ☐ **QE 22** ($15.95) Amanda Lohrey *Voting for Jesus*
- ☐ **QE 23** ($15.95) Inga Clendinnen *The History Question*
- ☐ **QE 24** ($15.95) Robyn Davidson *No Fixed Address*
- ☐ **QE 25** ($15.95) Peter Hartcher *Bipolar Nation*
- ☐ **QE 26** ($15.95) David Marr *His Master's Voice*
- ☐ **QE 27** ($15.95) Ian Lowe *Reaction Time*
- ☐ **QE 28** ($15.95) Judith Brett *Exit Right*
- ☐ **QE 29** ($16.95) Anne Manne *Love & Money*
- ☐ **QE 30** ($16.95) Paul Toohey *Last Drinks*
- ☐ **QE 31** ($16.95) Tim Flannery *Now or Never*
- ☐ **QE 32** ($16.95) Kate Jennings *American Revolution*
- ☐ **QE 33** ($17.95) Guy Pearse *Quarry Vision*
- ☐ **QE 34** ($17.95) Annabel Crabb *Stop at Nothing*
- ☐ **QE 35** ($17.95) Noel Pearson *Radical Hope*
- ☐ **QE 36** ($17.95) Mungo MacCallum *Australian Story*
- ☐ **QE 37** ($20.95) Waleed Aly *What's Right?*

Payment Details I enclose a cheque/money order made out to Schwartz Media Pty Ltd. Please debit my credit card (Mastercard or Visa accepted).

Card No. ☐☐☐☐ ☐☐☐☐ ☐☐☐☐ ☐☐☐☐

Expiry date   /   **Amount $**

Cardholder's name   **Signature**

Name

Address

Email

POST OR FAX THIS FORM TO: Quarterly Essay, Reply Paid 79448, Melbourne, VIC 3000 / Freecall: 1800 077 514 / Fax: 61 3 9654 2290 / Email: subscribe@blackincbooks.com

Subscribe online at **www.quarterlyessay.com**